THE
ATLANTIC
LINERS

THE
ATLANTIC
LINERS

FREDERICK EMMONS

Bonanza Books • New York

This edition is published by Bonanza Books,
distributed by Crown Publishers, Inc.,
by arrangement with Drake Publishers, Inc.

Manufactured in the United States of America

Library of Congress Cataloging in Publication Data
Emmons, Frederick.
  The Atlantic liners
  Originally published: New York : Drake Publishers,
1972.
  Bibliography: p.
  Includes index.
  1. Ocean liners—Registers.   I. Title.
HE566.025E45   1984   387.2'432   84-2793
ISBN: 0-517-209837

j i h g f e d c

CONTENTS

FOREWORD

It is not the purpose of this book to attempt a history of the North Atlantic liners, since the subject has been thoroughly covered in great detail in the past. Rather it is hoped that the illustrations and brief biographies of the various ships will serve to recall to ship-lovers and former passengers the appearance and characteristics of ships now vanished from the sea, and to serve as a comprehensive, if somewhat abbreviated record of all the ships in service on the Atlantic in the past forty-five years. In this connection, it seems pertinent to add a few words on the background of events which have made the Atlantic passenger trade the most populous and lucrative seaway in history.

Since the time of Columbus, men have braved the perils of the Western Ocean to find fame and fortune. The voyages of discovery and exploration were followed by the ships of the early colonists, whose numbers eventually swelled to the tide of emigrants which reached its flood in the early years of this century.

Of necessity, these people, over thirty million of them, travelled by ship. They came to the New World for many reasons, but essentially in search of a better life: to escape wars, famine, religious persecution and hopeless poverty. They lined the rails of the emigrant ships, straining for their first sight of the Statue of Liberty in New York harbour, and in 1907 alone, a million and a quarter of them poured through the lofty halls of the Immigration Station at Ellis Island to finally reach the promised land.

The outbreak of the First World War brought this emigrant flow to an abrupt and tragic halt, and at its end, the principal British steamship lines were sorely depleted by four years of U-boat warfare. The great pre-war German fleets were confiscated by the victorious Allies and vanished temporarily from the maritime scene.

There ensued a period of feverish construction activity to replace the lost tonnage and satisfy the renewed demand for shipping. However, the expectations upon which the post-war shipbuilding programmes were based were nullified by the passage in 1923 of the Dillingham Immigration Act setting quotas based on national origin and effectively marking the end of the mass emigrant movement. 1925 was therefore a year of change for the shipping lines of the North Atlantic. This loss of the immigrant trade was beginning to be offset by a movement in the opposite direction, the increasing tide of tourism. The character of the ships began to change accordingly. Another series of events was a tiny cloud on the shipping horizon: the early attempts to fly the Atlantic, highlighted by Charles Lindbergh's epic flight from New York to Paris in May of 1927, and the flight of the Graf Zeppelin a year later. Then, in the fall of 1929, the New York stock market crashed, to usher in a period of world-wide economic depression which was to have a devastating effect on shipping everywhere.

Nevertheless, the years between 1929 and 1935 were years of international competition for maritime prestige; the era of the highly publicized express liner. During this period, the Norddeutscher Lloyd liners BREMEN and EUROPA, Canadian Pacific's EMPRESS OF BRITAIN, the Italian Line's REX and CONTE DI SAVOIA, the French Line's NORMANDIE and Cunard's QUEEN MARY vied in turn as the latest, largest, fastest or most spectacularly luxurious.

The handwriting was on the wall however. In 1937 the first transatlantic mail service was begun, and two years later the world was once again at war; a war in which bombers were flown across the Atlantic regularly, and the wholesale sinkings began all over again. Of the seven magnificent express liners, only two survived.

The post-war period saw a build-up in tourist travel which increased year by year, more than doubling in a decade. But now a new factor had entered the picture. In the 1950s transatlantic passengers travelling by air increased from thirty to seventy percent of the total. In October 1958, the first Pan American jet took off from New York to bring the crossing time down to a few hours, and the jet age had begun.

The shipping companies, fighting for their existence, began to explore the possibilities of long-range cruising, made feasible by the increased leisure and wealth of the post-war prosperity. Unprofitable services were abandoned, older ships laid up, and new ships were adapted to cruising needs. Unfortunately for American-flag passenger shipping, never healthy economically despite government subsidies, the continuing upward spiral of costs eventually forced the transatlantic liners from the seas, and the "Blue Riband" holder UNITED STATES today lies idle at Newport News.

The 1970 Shipping Guide lists a total of 28 liners engaged in the North Atlantic trade, making a total of 286 crossings during the course of the year. However, just six ships sail on over half of these crossings, while no less then eight make but one round voyage during the year, usually incidental to their seasonal schedule of cruises.

Flying, though it can never match a sea voyage as a travel experience, has two obvious advantages: relatively low fares and greatly reduced travel time, and the airplane will certainly continue to carry people across the ocean in ever larger numbers. Today charter flights are available at even lower rates and presumably supersonic airliners will one day cut present flight times in half.

This competition, along with ever-increasing operational costs, threatens to mark the end of a maritime era. Passenger vessels being built today are designed for the requirements of long-range cruising service with emphasis on their function as floating resorts. The great Atlantic liners, like the clipper ships before them, are slowly being driven out of existence by the technology of our times.

Frederick Emmons
Los Angeles, California

EXPLANATORY NOTES

With the exception of a few ships of limited activity in the late 1920s, the List includes all passenger vessels in service in the North Atlantic since 1925. This would normally be equivalent to listing all Atlantic liners built in the twentieth century were it not for losses due to war and the hazards of the sea. The biggest omission, of course, is the considerable number of ships, mostly of British registry, sunk in the first World War.

Two famous liners, the TITANIC and LUSITANIA, are not included, but their appearance is indicated by the illustrations of their sister ships, the OLYMPIC and MAURETANIA. Also missing are the German ships which, for one reason or another, did not return to commercial service after World War I. Notable among these are the turn-of-the-century, four funnelled express liners, Norddeutscher Lloyd's KAISER WILHELM DER GROSSE, KRONPRINZ WILHELM, KAISER WILHELM II and KRONPRINZESSIN CECILE and the Hamburg American Line's DEUTSCHLAND. However, the surviving pre-war German ships, including the three Hamburg American giants, IMPERATOR, VATERLAND and BISMARCK are shown under the names given them by their new owners after the war.

Notes to each illustration contain the following information to the extent known:

1. Name of ship
2. Year Built
3. Years on Atlantic service
4. Gross registered tonnage
5. Overall length and breadth in feet. (R) indicates registered length.
6. Number of screws, type of engines, service speed
7. Name of builder
8. Ports of departure and arrival, and date of maiden voyage (M.V.), or first Atlantic voyage (F.V.)
9. Date and place of sinking or breaking up

Drawings are at a scale of one inch equals 160 feet.　● Beside name indicates ship in service in 1971.

1 GREAT BRITAIN

CUNARD LINE, SOUTHAMPTON (1840-   )

The Cunard Steam-Ship Co Ltd, the oldest, largest and the most famous company on the North Atlantic, was founded in 1838 by a partnership headed by Samuel Cunard, a Nova Scotia merchant. Four steamers were ordered for the service, and the first sailing was taken by the wooden paddle steamer BRITANNIA which left Liverpool for Halifax and Boston, 4 July 1840.

As the service prospered over the years, the fleet was greatly expanded. At the turn of the century however, the Company had but eight ships in the trade; less than at any time in the past fifty years. A new building programme was begun which included the construction of the LUSITANIA and MAURETANIA, two ships of advanced design and the fastest yet built.

With the outbreak of World War I, the Company's ships were taken over for war service, carrying over a million troops as well as huge quantities of supplies No less than nine Cunard passenger ships were sunk by enemy action, including the LUSITANIA which was torpedoed off the Irish coast with the loss of nearly 1200 lives.

After the war, the Line acquired the ex-German liner IMPERATOR, which was renamed BERENGARIA, and a massive programme of new construction resulted in the commissioning of thirteen new vessels in the period 1921-25. In 1930, work was begun on a new super-liner, but construction was halted by the world economic depression. It was finally resumed in 1934 with a government loan made contingent upon amalgamation of the Company with the White Star Line. The new ship, the QUEEN MARY, went into service in 1936 followed by a consort, the QUEEN ELIZABETH, four years later.

Again in 1939 the Line's nineteen ships served in the war effort. At the end of hostilities only nine were available for use, five of the remainder having been sunk. In the next few years seven new ships were added to the fleet.

In 1962 the SAXONIA and IVERNIA were refitted as cruise ships and renamed CARMANIA and FRANCONIA, and as the transatlantic passenger trade declined in the 1960s, the MAURITANIA (II) was broken up and the remaining seven passenger ships of the fleet, including the "Queens", were sold. In 1969 the flagship QUEEN ELIZABETH 2, possibly the last great Atlantic liner, was placed in transatlantic express service and has since operated alone, while the CARMANIA and FRANCONIA continue to be engaged primarily in cruising.

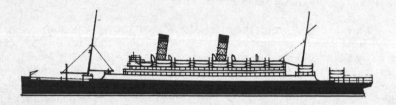

1 CARONIA (I)

'05, (1905-32) 19,594. 678 x 72. Twin screw, quadruple expansion engines, 19 knots. Built by John Brown & Co, Clydebank, Glasgow. M.V. Liverpool - New York, 25 February 1905. Commissioned as armed merchant cruiser 1914; converted to troop ship 1916. Resumed passenger service January 1919. Sold to Japanese ship-breakers 1932. Sailed to Japan as TAISEIYO MARU; broken up Osaka 1933.

2 CARMANIA (I)

'05.(1905-32) 19,524. 678 x 72. Triple screw, turbines, 18 knots. Built by John Brown & Co. M.V. Liverpool - New York, 2 December 1905. Took a leading part in the rescue of passengers and crew from the burning British liner VOLTURNO in the North Atlantic, 9 October 1913. Commissioned as armed merchant cruiser 1914. Engaged and sank the armed German liner CAP TRAFALGAR off Trinidad Island, 14 September 1914. Resumed passenger service December 1918. Broken up Blyth 1932.

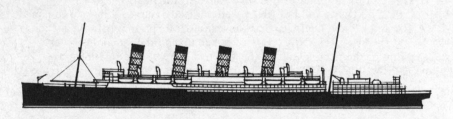

3 MAURETANIA (I)

'07, (1907-35) 31,938. 790 x 88. Quadruple screw, turbines, 26 knots. Built by Swan, Hunter & Wigham Richardson, Wallsend-on-Tyne; a sister ship of the LUSITANIA. M.V. Liverpool - New York, 16 November 1907. Return Eastbound crossing made at an average speed of 23.69 knots for a new speed record. Holder of the "Blue Riband" of the North Atlantic for twenty years, she was one of the most famous and successful of Atlantic liners. Served as troopship and hospital ship 1915-19. Broken up Rosyth 1935.

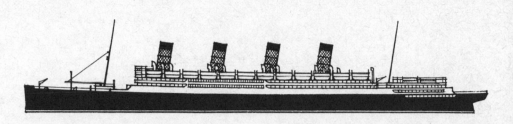

4 AQUITANIA

'14, (1914-49) 45,647. 902 x 97. Quadruple screw, turbines, 24 knots. Built by John Brown & Co, Clydebank, Glasgow. M.V. Liverpool-New York, 30 May 1914. The last four-funnelled Atlantic liner, considered by many to be one of the most beautiful ships ever built. Commissioned as armed merchant cruiser, August 1914, after only three voyages. Served as hospital ship and troopship 1915-19, and again as troopship 1939-48; the only great liner to serve in both wars. Partially refitted to carry war brides and emigrants to Canada 1948-49. Withdrawn from service December 1949 after having steamed nearly 3,000,000 miles and carried an estimated 1,200,000 passengers. Broken up Faslane 1950.

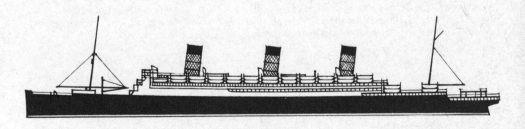

5 BERENGARIA

'13, (1921-38) 52,002, 919 x 98. Quadruple screw, turbines, 23 knots. Built by A.G.Vulkan, Hamburg, as IMPERATOR for Hamburg American Line. M.V. Hamburg - New York, 18 June 1913. Laid up in Elbe River 1914-19. Acquired by Cunard Line 1920, renamed BERENGARIA 1921. F.V. Southampton - New York, 16 April 1921. Refitted on Tyne 1922; converted to fuel oil. Damaged by fire at New York, March 1938. Hull dismantled to waterline at Jarrow later in year; remains finally broken up Rosyth 1946.

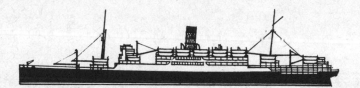

6 SCYTHIA (II)

'21, (1921-57) 19,730. 624 x 73. Twin screw, turbines, 16 knots. Built by Vickers-Armstrongs, Barrow-in-Furness. Due to labour disputes moved to L'Orient, France for completion. M.V. Liverpool-New York, 21 August 1921. Converted to troopship 1939. Resumed regular passenger service September 1950. Broken up Inverkeithing 1958.

7 SAMARIA (II)

'22, (1922-55) 19,602. Details as (6). Built by Cammell Laird & Co, Birkenhead. M.V. Liverpool-Boston, 19 April 1922. Converted to troopship 1939. Resumed regular passenger service June 1951. Broken up Inverkeithing 1956.

8 LACONIA (II)

'22, (1922-42) 19,680. Details as (6). Built by Swan, Hunter & Wigham Richardson, Wallsend-on-Tyne. M.V. Southampton - New York, 25 May 1922. Commissioned as armed merchant cruiser 1939 but converted to troopship the following year. Torpedoed and sunk by German submarine U-156 in South Atlantic while carrying Italian prisoners of war, with loss of nearly two thirds of the 2,700 persons aboard, 12 September 1942. Five days after sinking, French cruiser GLOIRE arrived and took survivors to Dakar.

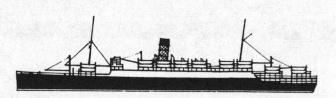

9 LANCASTRIA

'22, (1922-40) 16,243. 578 x 70. Twin screw, turbines, 15 knots. Built by Wm. Beardmore & Co, Glasgow, as TYRRHENIA. M.V. Glasgow - Montreal, 13 June 1922. Renamed LANCASTRIA 1924. Engaged in cruising service after 1932. Converted to troopship 1939. Sunk by German dive bombers while crammed with an estimated 9,000 British troops being evacuated from St Nazaire, 17 June 1940. Direct hits by four heavy bombs resulted in the loss of more than half of the embarked troops.

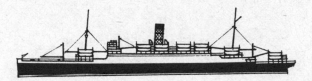

10 ANDANIA (II)
'22, (1922-40) 13,950. 540 x 65. Twin screw, turbines, 15 knots. Built by R & W Hawthorn, Leslie & Co, Hebburn-on -Tyne. M.V. Southampton - Montreal, 1 June 1922. Commissioned as armed merchant cruiser 1939. Torpedoed and sunk near Iceland, 15 June 1940.

11 ANTONIA
'22, (1922-42) 13,867. Details as (10). Built by Vickers-Armstrongs. M.V. Southampton-Montreal, 15 June 1922. Commissioned as armed merchant cruiser 1940. Sold to British Admiralty 1942. Converted to repair ship 1944; renamed H M S WAYLAND. Broken up Scotland 1948.

12 AUSONIA (II)
'22, (1922-42) 13,912. Details as (10). Built by Sir W.G. Armstrong, Whitworth & Co, Newcastle. M.V. Liverpool - Montreal, 22 June 1922. Commissioned as armed merchant cruiser 1939. Sold to British Admiralty 1942; converted to heavy repair ship 1944. Laid up at end of war, but recommissioned 1958 as repair ship for Mediterranean fleet stationed at Malta. Broken up Castellon, Spain 1965.

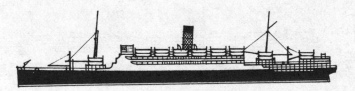

13 FRANCONIA (II)
'23, (1923-56) 20,158. 624 x 73. Twin screw, turbines, 16 knots. Built by John Brown & Co, Clydebank, Glasgow. M.V. Liverpool-New York, 23 June 1923. Famous winter cruise liner. Converted to troopship 1939. Resumed passenger service June 1949. Broken up Inverkeithing 1956.

14 CARINTHIA (I)
'25, (1925-40) 20,277. Details as (13). Laid down as SERVIA by Vickers-Armstrongs, Barrow-in-Furness, but renamed before launching. M.V. Liverpool-New York, 22 August 1925. Commissioned as armed merchant cruiser 1939. Torpedoed and sunk off the coast of Northern Ireland, 6 June 1940.

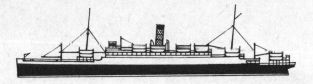

15 AURANIA (III)
'24, (1924-42) 13,984. 540 x 65. Twin screw, turbines, 15 knots. Built by Swan, Hunter & Wigham Richardson, Wallsend-on-Tyne. M.V. Liverpool-New York, 13 September 1924. Commissioned as armed merchant cruiser 1939. Sold to British Admiralty 1942. Converted to repair ship 1944; renamed H M S ARTIFEX. Broken up La Spezia 1961.

16 ASCANIA (II)
'25, (1925-56) 14,013. Details as (15). Built by Sir W.G. Armstrong, Whitworth & Co, Newcastle. M.V. London-Montreal, 22 May 1925. Commissioned as armed merchant cruiser 1939; later converted to troopship. Resumed passenger service December 1947. Broken up Newport 1957.

17 ALAUNIA (II)
'25, (1925-44) 14,030. Details as (15). Built by John Brown & Co, Clydebank, Glasgow. M.V. Liverpool-Montreal, 24 July 1925. Commissioned as armed merchant cruiser 1939. Sold to British Admiralty 1944, converted to repair ship. Broken up Blyth 1957.

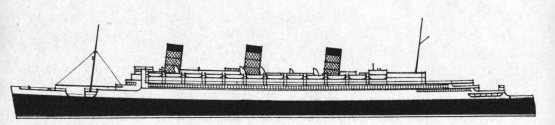

18 QUEEN MARY
'36, (1936-67) 81,237. 1,020 x 118. Quadruple screw, turbines, 29 knots. Laid down 1930 by John Brown & Co. Work suspended late 1931 due to economic depression; resumed April 1934. M.V. Southampton - New York, 27 May 1936. Became undisputed holder of the "Blue Riband" in August 1938 with crossings at speeds of 30.99 knots westbound and 31.69 knots eastbound; a record held until 1952. Laid up at New York at outbreak of war; converted to troopship at Sydney, Australia 1940. In collision with escorting cruiser H M S CURACAO which sank with loss of 329 lives, 2 October 1942. Resumed passenger service, July 1947. Sold to City of Long Beach, California for conversion to floating museum and hotel; delivered after voyage around Cape Horn, December 1967.

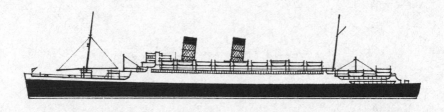

19 MAURETANIA (II)
'39, (1939-65) 35,738. 771 x 89. Twin screw, turbines, 22 knots. Built by Cammell, Laird & Co, Birkenhead. M.V. Liverpool - New York, 17 June 1939. Laid up at New York December 1939. Converted to troopship at Sydney 1940. Resumed passenger service 26 April 1947. Broken up Inverkeithing 1965.

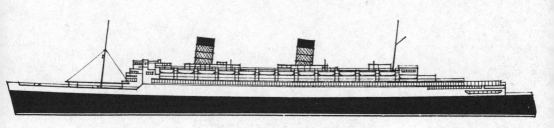

20 QUEEN ELIZABETH
'40, (1946-68) 83,673. 1,031 x 118. Quadruple screw, turbines, 29 knots. Built by John Brown & Co, Clydebank, Glasgow; the largest passenger ship in the world. Left the Clyde for New York under wartime conditions, 27 February 1940. Served as troopship 1940-46. Refitted for passenger service 1946; F.V. Southampton - New York, 16 October 1946. Sold for use as exhibit and convention centre at Fort Lauderdale, Florida, 1968. Sold to Orient Overseas Line 1970, renamed SEAWISE UNIVERSITY and registered in Bahamas. Refitted for cruising and schoolship service at Hong Kong 1971.

21 MEDIA
'41, (1947-61) 13,345.531 x 70. Twin screw, turbines, 18 knots. Built by John Brown & Co,
Clydebank, Glasgow. M.V. Liverpool - New York, 20 August 1947. Sold to Cogedar Line (Italy)
1961; extensively refitted at Genoa and renamed FLAVIA. Sold to Costa Line (Italy) for cruising
service 1968.

22 PARTHIA (II)
'48, (1948-61) 13.362. Details as (21). Built by Harland & Wolff, Belfast. M.V. Liverpool - New
York, 10 April 1948. Sold to New Zealand Shipping Co, (Great Britain) 1961; refitted at Glasgow
and renamed REMUERA. Transferred to Eastern & Australian Steamship Co, (Great Britain) 1964;
renamed ARAMAC. Broken up Kaohsiung, Taiwan 1969.

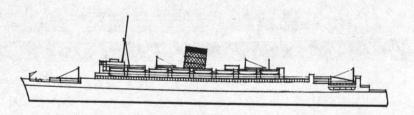

23 CARONIA (II)
'48, (1949-67) 34,274. 715 x 91. Twin screw, turbines, 24 knots. Built by John Brown & Co,
M.V. Southampton - New York, 4 January 1949. Extensively engaged in cruising. Withdrawn from
service November 1967. Sold to Universal Cruise Line (Panama) 1968; renamed COLUMBIA, later
CARIBIA. Laid up at New York 1969.

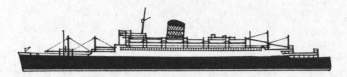

24 SAXONIA (II)
'54, (1954-62) 21,657. 608 x 80 Twin screw, turbines, 20 knots. Built by John Brown & Co, Clydebank, Glasgow. M.V. Liverpool-Montreal, 2 September 1954. Renamed CARMANIA (28) 1963.

25 IVERNIA (II)
'55, (1955-62) 21,717. Details as (24). Built by John Brown & Co, M.V. Greenock - Montreal, 1 July 1955. Renamed FRANCONIA (29) 1963.

26 CARINTHIA (II)
'56, (1956-68) 21,947. Details as (24). Built by John Brown & Co. M.V. Liverpool - Montreal, 27 June 1956. Laid up at Southampton November 1967. Sold to Sitmar Line (Liberia) 1968; renamed FAIRLAND, later FAIRSEA.

27 SYLVANIA
'57, (1957-68) 22,017.Details as (24). Built by John Brown & Co. M.V. Liverpool-Montreal, 26 June 1957. Laid up at Southampton May 1968. Sold to Sitmar Line 1968; renamed FAIRWIND.

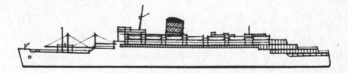

28 CARMANIA (II) ●
'54, (1963-   ) 21,370.Formerly SAXONIA (24) Cunard Line . Refitted for cruising service 1963; renamed CARMANIA.

29 FRANCONIA (III) ●
'55, (1963-) 21,406. Formerly IVERNIA (25) Cunard Line. Refitted for cruising service 1963; renamed FRANCONIA.

19

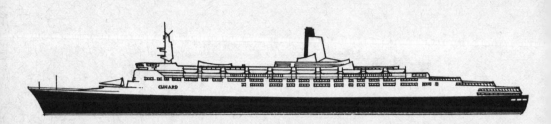

30 QUEEN ELIZABETH 2 ●
'68, (1969-) 65,863. 963 x 105. Twin-screw, turbines, 28 knots. Built by John Brown & Co,
Clydebank, Glasgow. Left Greenock on shakedown cruise to Canary Islands, 23 December 1968.
Acceptance delayed as a result of turbine troubles; F.V. Southampton-New York, 2 May 1969.

ANCHOR LINE, GLASGOW (1856-1940)

The Anchor Line, the oldest Scottish steamship company, was founded by the Glasgow firm of Handyside & Henderson to provide shipping for the North American trade. The initial sailing on 11 October 1856 was by the 886 ton iron screw steamer TEMPEST, the first of a long line of Anchor ships. In the 1880s the Line prospered, transporting the waves of emigrants from Scotland and northern Europe to the New World.

Losses in World War I were heavy, the COLUMBIA being the only survivor of the Line's six Atlantic liners. Five new ships were laid down in a post-war building programme, but the American immigration restrictions of the 1920s made serious inroads in the Company's business, and construction of the TRANSYLVANIA and CALEDONIA was suspended for two years.

The economic depression of the next decade had a further adverse financial effect. The CAMERONIA was laid up for a time, while the TUSCANIA was chartered to the Cunard Line for five years during the summer months, operating on the Line's Bombay service in winter. In 1939 the TUSCANIA was sold to the Greek Line, and soon afterward three of the four remaining ships were requisitioned by the Admiralty for war duty as armed merchant cruisers and were eventually lost through enemy action.

The last Atlantic crossing was taken by the CAMERONIA late in 1940, and although she survived the war, the service was never resumed.

31 COLUMBIA (II)
'02, (1902-26) 8,292. 502 x 46. Twin screw, triple expansion engines, 15 knots. Built by D & W
Henderson & Co, Glasgow. M.V. Glasgow-New York, 17 May 1902. Commissioned as armed
merchant cruiser H M S COLUMBELLA in 10th Cruiser Squadron 1914-19. Sold to Byron Line
(Great Britain) 1926; renamed MOREAS (225). Transferred to National Steam Navigation Co,
of Greece, 1928.

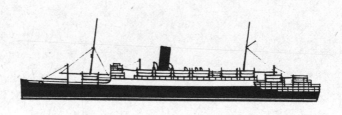

32 CAMERONIA (II)
'21, (1921-40) 16,365. 575 x 70. Twin screw, turbines, 15 knots. Built by Wm. Beardmore & Co,
Glasgow. M.V. Liverpool-New York, 11 May 1921. Laid up in the Clyde, December 1934. Served
as troopship 1935-36. Sailed on wartime trooping service January 1941. Disabled by aerial torpedo
off North African coast December 1942; repaired on the Clyde. Refitted for emigrant service to
Australia 1948. Sold to British Ministry of Transport 1953 for service as troopship; renamed
EMPIRE CLYDE. Broken up Newport 1957.

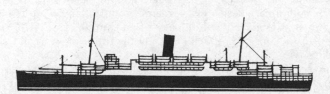

33 TUSCANIA (II)
'22, (1922-39) 16,991. 575 x 70. Twin screw, turbines, 16 knots. Built by Fairfield Shipbuilding & Engineering Co, Govan, Glasgow. M.V. Glasgow-New York, 16 September 1922. Chartered by Cunard Line 1926-30 for summer service; later employed in Liverpool-India service and cruising. Sold to Greek Line 1939; renamed NEA HELLAS (226).

34 CALIFORNIA (III)
'23, (1923-43) 16,792. Details as (33). Built by Alexander Stephen & Sons, Linthouse, Glasgow. M.V. Glasgow-New York, 26 August 1923. Commissioned as armed merchant cruiser 1939. Converted to troopship 1942. Bombed and sunk off Cape St Vincent, 11 July 1943.

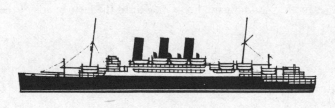

35 TRANSYLVANIA (II)
'25, (1925-40) 16,923. 575 x 70. Twin screw, turbines, 15 knots. Built by Fairfield Shipbuilding & Engineering Co, M.V. Glasgow - New York, 12 September 1925. Commissioned as armed merchant cruiser 1939. Torpedoed and sunk west of the Hebrides, 10 August 1940.

36 CALEDONIA (IV)
'25, (1925-40) 17,046. Details as (35). Built by Alexander Stephen & Sons. M.V. Glasgow - New York, 3 October 1925. Commissioned as armed merchant cruiser 1939; renamed H M S SCOTSTOUN. Torpedoed and sunk off Northern Ireland, 13 June 1940.

WHITE STAR LINE, LIVERPOOL (1871-1934)

The Oceanic Steam Navigation Co, known as the White Star Line, was founded by Thomas Ismay in 1869, ostensibly to provide shipping services to Australia. Six new steamers of revolutionary design were ordered from Harland & Wolff for the purpose. However, in a surprise move, the Company's first ship, the OCEANIC, sailed from Liverpool for New York on 2 March 1871. By the following year all six ships were in transatlantic service.

After the second OCEANIC was commissioned in 1899, the line adopted a policy of building large, extremely comfortable ships of moderate speed. This influenced the design of her successors, the CELTIC, CEDRIC, BALTIC and ADRIATIC, which became famous as the "Big Four".

In 1902 the International Mercantile Marine Co was formed and purchased control of the Line along with a number of other companies. Due to its prestige, the White Star was favoured within the group, and one early result was its acquisition of four new Dominion Line steamers.

The pre-World War I period was marked by the most tragic peace-time sea disaster in history when the Line's largest ship, the TITANIC, struck an iceberg while on her maiden voyage in April 1912 and sank with a loss of over 1500 lives. War service resulted in additional losses, including the liners ARABIC, LAURENTIC and the new 48,000 ton BRITANNIC. As replacements, the line acquired three ex-German vessels, including the unfinished BISMARCK which was completed as the MAJESTIC, the largest ship in the world.

The depression of the early 1930s resulted in the disposal of a number of ships, while others were employed on cruises. In deep financial trouble, the Line was merged with the Cunard Line in 1934 to form Cunard-White Star Ltd, and although the Cunard Line assumed control of the organisation, the White Star ships retained their funnel markings and house flag until the last voyage of the BRITANNIC in 1960.

37 CELTIC (II)
'01, (1901-28) 20,904. 697 x 75. Twin screw, quadruple expansion engines, 16 knots. Built by
Harland & Wolff, Belfast. M.V. Liverpool - New York, 26 July 1901. Converted to troopship
1915. Resumed passenger sailings December 1918. Went aground off Cobh, 10 December 1928.
and became a total loss. Broken up where she lay 1933.

38 CEDRIC
'03, (1903-31) 21,035. Details as (37). Built by Harland & Wolff. M.V. Liverpool - New York, 11
February 1903. Commissioned as armed merchant cruiser in 10th Cruiser Squadron, December
1914. Served as troopship 1915-18. Broken up Inverkeithing 1932.

39 CANOPIC
'00, (1904-25) 12,097. 594 x 59. Twin screw, triple expansion engines, 16 knots. Built by Harland
& Wolff as COMMONWEALTH for Dominion Line. Transferred to White Star Line 1903;
renamed CANOPIC. F.V. Liverpool - Boston, 14 January 1904. Served as troopship 1914-18.
Broken up Briton Ferry, South Wales, 1925.

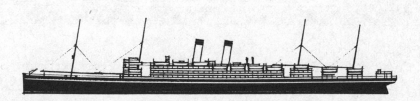

40 BALTIC (II)
'04, (1904-33) 23,876. 726 x 76. Twin screw, quadruple expansion engines, 16 knots. Built by
Harland & Wolff, Belfast. M.V. Liverpool-New York, 29 June 1904. Broken up Osaka 1933.

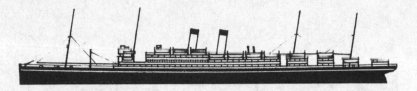

41 ADRIATIC (II)
'07, (1907-34) 24,541. 726 x 75. Twin screw, quadruple expansion engines, 17 knots. Built by Harland & Wolff. M.V. Liverpool - New York, 8 May 1907. The last of White Star Line's "Big Four". Broken up Osaka 1935.

42 MEGANTIC
'09, (1909-33) 14,878. 570 x 67. Twin screw, quadruple expansion engines, 16 knots. Laid down by Harland & Wolff, Belfast as ALBANY for Dominion Line; transferred to White Star Line and renamed MEGANTIC during construction. M.V. Liverpool - Montreal, 16 June 1909. Converted to troopship 1914; returned to passenger service December 1918. Laid up in Rothesay Bay, July 1931; broken up Osaka 1933.

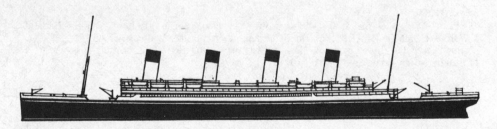

43 OLYMPIC
'11,(1911-35) 46,439. 883 x 92. Triple screw, combination triple expansion engines and turbine, 23 knots. Built by Harland & Wolff. M.V. Southampton - New York, 14 June 1911. Badly damaged in collision with cruiser H M S HAWKE off Portsmouth, 20 September 1911. Extensively rebuilt after loss of sister TITANIC in 1912. Converted to troopship September 1915. Rammed and sank German submarine U-103, 12 May 1918. Resumed passenger service July 1920. Transferred to Cunard - White Star Line 1934. Rammed and sank Nantucket Lightship with all hands during thick fog, 16 May 1934. Withdrawn from service and partially broken up Jarrow 1935; towed to Inverkeithing for final demolition 1937.

44 ARABIC (III)
'08, (1921-31) 16,786. 615 x 69. Twin screw, quadruple expansion engines, 17 knots. Built by A. G. Weser, Bremen, as BERLIN for Norddeutscher Lloyd. Converted to auxiliary minelayer cruiser 1914; laid minefield off Northern Ireland which sank British battleship H M S AUDACIOUS. Interned at Trondheim, Norway, for remainder of war. Allocated to Great Britain as war reparation; acquired by White Star Line 1920. Refitted at Portsmouth 1921; renamed ARABIC. F.V. Southampton-New York, 7 September 1921. Transferred to Red Star Line 1925-29. Returned to White Star service March 1930, but laid up later in year. Broken up Italy 1931.

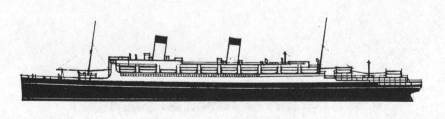

45 HOMERIC
'22, (1922-35) 34,351. 774 x 83. Twin screw, triple expansion engines, 19 knots. Launched in 1913 by F. Schichau, Danzig, as COLUMBUS for Norddeutscher Lloyd; construction delayed by war. Allocated to British Government as reparation 1920. Bought by White Star Line and completed 1921; renamed HOMERIC. M.V. Southampton-New York, 15 February 1922. The largest ship on the North Atlantic with twin screws and reciprocating engines. Employed exclusively in cruising after 1932. Transferred to Cunard-White Star Line 1934. Laid up in Southampton Water, September 1935; broken up Inverkeithing 1936.

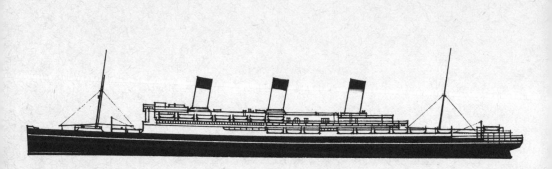

46 MAJESTIC (II)
'22.(1922-36) 56,551. 956 x 100. Quadruple screw, turbines, 24 knots. Launched 1914 by Blohm
& Voss, Hamburg; as BISMARCK for Hamburg American Line; construction suspended during
war. Ceded to British Government as war reparation; bought by White Star Line 1921.
Construction completed March 1922; renamed MAJESTIC. M.V. Southampton-New York, 10 May
1922. Transferred to Cunard-White Star Line in 1934. Sold to British Admiralty 1936 and
converted to boys' training ship; renamed HMS CALEDONIA. Gutted by fire and sank at Rosyth,
29 September 1939. Refloated and towed to Inverkeithing for demolition 1943.

47 DORIC
'23,(1923-35) 16,484. 601 x 68. Twin screw, turbines, 17 knots. Built by Harland & Wolff,
Belfast. M.V. Liverpool-Montreal, 6 July 1923. After 1933 engaged in cruising. Transferred to
Cunard-White Star Line in 1934. Seriously damaged in collision with French steamer FORMIGNY
off coast of Portugal, 5 September 1935. Made port at Vigo for temporary repairs before returning
to England; broken up at Newport.

48 ALBERTIC
'23,(1927-34) 18,940. Formerly OHIO (101) Royal Mail. Transferred to White Star Line 1927; renamed ALBERTIC. F.V. Liverpool-Montreal, 22 April 1927. Laid up in Holy Loch, March 1933; broken up Osaka 1934.

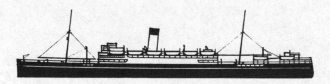

49 CALGARIC
'18, (1927-33) 16,063. Formerly ORCA (100) Royal Mail. Transferred to White Star Line 1927; renamed CALGARIC. F.V. Liverpool-Montreal, 4 May 1927. Laid up at Milford Haven, September 1933; broken up Rosyth 1935.

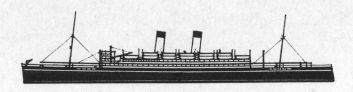

50 LAURENTIC
'27,(1927-40) 18,724. 603 x 75. Triple screw, combination triple expansion engines and turbine, 16 knots. Built by Harland & Wolff, Belfast; the last coal-burning transatlantic liner. M.V. Liverpool-New York, 12 November 1927. Transferred to Cunard-White Star Line 1934. Collided with NAPIER STAR in Irish Sea, 18 August 1935 with loss of six lives. Laid up after 1936 except for occasional cruises and charters for trooping. Commissioned as armed merchant cruiser 1939. Torpedoed and sunk off Bloody Foreland, 3 November 1940.

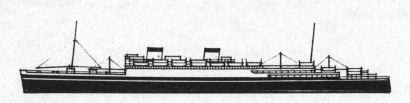

51 BRITANNIC
'30, (1930-60) 27,778. 712 x 82. Twin screw, motor ship, 18 knots. Built by Harland & Wolff, M.V. Liverpool-New York, 28 June 1930. Transferred to Cunard-White Star Line 1934. Converted to troopship 1939; passenger service not resumed until May 1948. Broken up Inverkeithing 1961.

52 GEORGIC
'32,(1932-41) (1950-54) 27,759. Details as (51). Built by Harland & Wolff. M.V. Liverpool-New York, 25 June 1932. Transferred to Cunard-White Star Line 1934. Converted to troopship 1940. Bombed and gutted off Port Tewfik, Egypt, 14 July 1941; temporarily repaired at Bombay. Rebuilt at Belfast as troopship and emigrant carrier by Ministry of Transport; main-mast and forward funnel removed. Chartered for transatlantic service by Cunard-White Star Line 1950-54. Broken up Faslane 1956.

DOMINION LINE, LIVERPOOL (1872-1926)

The Liverpool & Mississippi Steamship Co inaugurated a shipping service to New Orleans in 1870, and two years later began sending ships to Montreal in the summer months when the southern trade was slack. The first of these sailings from Liverpool was taken by the 2,000 ton steamer MISSISSIPPI on 4 May 1872. The Gulf service gradually declined, and the Company, turning to the Canadian trade, changed its name to the Mississippi & Dominion Steamship Co and eventually became known as the Dominion Line. In 1896 the CANADA, the Line's largest and most luxurious ship, inaugurated a new service to Boston, and by the turn of the century this port became the Company's principal western terminal.

The Company was bought by the International Mercantile Marine Co in 1902 and as a result its four largest ships, the NEW ENGLAND, COMMONWEALTH, MAY-FLOWER and COLUMBUS, were transferred to the White Star Line's Boston service as the ROMANIC, CANOPIC, CRETIC and REPUBLIC respectively.

The last ship built for the Line was the REGINA, completed in 1922. With her transfer to the White Star Line four years later, the Dominion Line's services came to an end.

53 CANADA
'96, (1896-1926) 9,413. 514 x 58. Twin screw, triple expansion engines, 15 knots. Built by Harland & Wolff, Belfast; the first twin-screw steamship for the Canadian service. M.V. Liverpool-Montreal, 1 November 1896. Served as troopship in Boer War, 1899-1902, and again in World War I, 1914-18. Broken up Italy 1926.

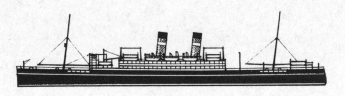

54 REGINA
'18, (1922-30) 16,313. 601 x 67. Triple screw, combination triple expansion engines and turbine, 16 knots. Laid down 1914 by Harland & Wolff; construction halted by war. Hastily completed as troopship without intended superstructure and with single funnel 1918. Refitted for passenger service 1922; F.V. Liverpool-Halifax, 16 March 1922. First ship to establish a new type of accommodation between Cabin and Third Class, later widely adopted as Tourist Class. Transferred to White Star Line 1926. Transferred to Red Star Line 1930; renamed WESTERNLAND (59).

RED STAR LINE, ANTWERP (1873-1935)

The Red Star Line was formed in Antwerp under the ownership of the Societe Anonyme de Navigation Belge-Americaine, a subsidiary of an American company, the International Navigation Co. The first sailing from Antwerp to Philadelphia was made by the Belgian flag, iron screw steamer VADERLAND on 19 January 1873. Within a few years however, the western terminal was shifted to New York.

In the 1890s the Line was operated in conjunction with the American Line whose ships were registered under both the British and American flags. When orders were placed in 1900 for four new ships, two, the VADERLAND and ZEELAND were British built and registered, while the KROONLAND and FINLAND were built and registered in the United States.

In 1902 the International Navigation Co became the International Mercantile Marine Co, a huge shipping trust which controlled a number of major steamship companies, including the Red Star. These lines retained their identities, although their ships were constantly interchanged.

During the German occupation of Antwerp in World War I, all the Company's ships except the emigrant ships GOTHLAND and SAMLAND were transferred from Belgian to British or American registry, and in the post-war years the fleet became almost entirely British.

In 1934, after a period of steady decline, only the WESTERNLAND and PENNLAND remained in operation. The following year they were sold to the Arnold Bernstein Co of Hamburg, together with the Red Star name and good will.

55 ZEELAND

'01, (1901-15) (1920-27) 11,905. 508 x 60. Twin screw, quadruple expansion engines, 15 knots.
Built by John Brown & Co, Clydebank, Glasgow. Transferred to Belgian registry 1902. In service
of White Star Line 1910-11. Returned to British registry 1915; renamed NORTHLAND. Served as
troopship in World War I. Resumed passenger service for Red Star Line, August 1920; renamed
ZEELAND. Transferred to Atlantic Transport Line 1927; renamed MINNESOTA (63).

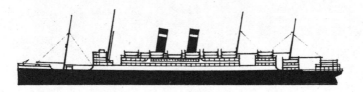

56 LAPLAND

'09, (1909-34) 17,540. 620 x 70. Twin screw, quadruple expansion engines, 18 knots. Built by
Harland & Wolff, Belfast. Registered in Belgium. M.V. Antwerp-New York, 10 April 1909. Transferred
to British registry after capture of the Port of Antwerp by the Germans 1914. Employed in White Star
service 1914-19. Resumed passenger service for Red Star Line January 1920; engaged in cruising
after 1931. Broken up Osaka 1934.

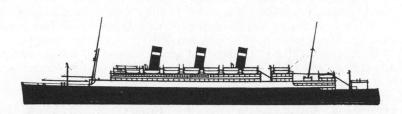

57 BELGENLAND

'17, (1923-34) 27,132. 696 x 78. Triple screw, combination triple expansion engines and turbine, 17 knots. Launched 1914 by Harland & Wolff, Belfast; work suspended at outbreak of war. Completed 1917 as troopship BELGIC operating under White Star management. Rebuilt to original design 1922 and returned to Red Star Line; renamed BELGENLAND. F.V. Antwerp - New York, 14 April 1923. Laid up at Antwerp 1932; placed in cruising service the following summer. Transferred to Panama Pacific Line (United States) 1934; renamed COLUMBIA. Broken up Bo'ness 1936.

58 PENNLAND

'22, (1926-40) 16,322. 601 x 67. Triple screw, combination triple expansion engines and turbine, 16 knots. Laid down 1913 by Harland & Wolff as PITTSBURGH for American Line (United States). Taken over by White Star Line during construction; completed 1922. Transferred to Red Star Line 1925. Renamed PENNLAND 1926. Sold to Arnold Bernstein 1935; service continued under Bernstein (Red Star) Line (Germany). Sold to Holland-America Line 1939. Chartered to British Government 1940; converted to troopship. Sunk by German bombers in Gulf of Athens while attempting to evacuate British troops from Greece, 25 April 1941.

59 WESTERNLAND

'22, (1930-40) 16,289. Formerly REGINA (54) Dominion Line. Transferred to White Star Line 1926. Transferred to Red Star Line 1930; renamed WESTERNLAND. Sold to Arnold Bernstein 1935. Sold to Holland-America Line 1939. Sailed to England and converted to troopship after invasion of Holland. Served as General de Gaulle's flagship in attack on Dakar, August 1941. Laid up at London, November 1942; broken up Blyth 1947.

ATLANTIC TRANSPORT LINE, NEW YORK (1892-1932)

The Atlantic Transport Line started operations in 1882 as a cargo service between Baltimore and London. For reasons of economy its ships were registered under the British flag. A few years later, it was decided to enter the London-New York passenger trade and the service was begun in 1892 with two new twin-screw steamers, the MANITOBA and MASSACHUSETTS. The fleet was increased to five in the next five years, only to be purchased by the United States Government in 1898 for use as transports in the Spanish-American War.

Replacements were obtained by the purchase of five ships of the Wilson's & Furness-Leyland Line. Within a few months, one of them, the MOHEGAN, was lost on the coast of Cornwall with a death toll of 106.

In 1902 the Line, along with a number of others was purchased by the International Mercantile Marine Co, an event which involved a considerable number of transfers between the various members of the group. Two years earlier the Line had commissioned the MINNEAPOLIS and MINNEHAHA which were later followed by the MINNETONKA and MINNEWASKA. These ships were extremely popular, with spacious accommodations and immense cargo capacity. All four were sunk in World War I.

Post-war replacements to the fleet included a new MINNEWASKA and MINNETONKA as well as the refitted MINNEKAHDA which had been completed as a cargo vessel during the war.

The MINNESOTA was sold for breaking up in 1929 and, as a result of the depression in the early 1930s, the rest of the Line's passenger ships were disposed of within the next three years to mark the end of the Company's existence.

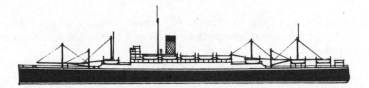

60 MINNEKAHDA

'17, (1921-36) 17,221. 646 x 66. Triple screw, combination triple expansion engines and turbine, 16 knots. Laid down 1914 by Harland & Wolff, Belfast, as two-funnelled intermediate liner Construction delayed by war; completed as cargo ship without superstructure 1917. Transferred to American registry 1920; refitted to carry over 2,000 emigrant passengers at Quincy, Massachusetts. Assigned to American Line (United States) 1921. F.V. New York-Hamburg, 31 March 1921. Transferred to Atlantic Transport Line 1924; converted to tourist class ship. Laid up at New York 1931; broken up Dalmuir 1936.

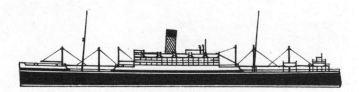

61 MINNEWASKA (IV)

'23, (1923-34) 21,716. 626 x 80. Twin screw, turbines, 16 knots. Built by Harland & Wolff. M.V. London-New York, 1 September 1923. Transferred to Red Star Line 1932. Broken up Port Glasgow 1934.

62 MINNETONKA (II)

'24, (1924-34) 21,988. Details as (61). Built by Harland & Wolff. M.V. London-New York, 3 May 1924. Transferred to Red Star Line 1932. Broken up Bo'ness 1934.

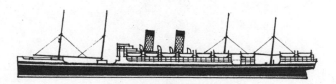

63 MINNESOTA (II)

'01, (1927-20) 11,667. Formerly ZEELAND (55) Red Star Line. Transferred to Atlantic Transport Line 1927; renamed MINNESOTA. Broken up Inverkeithing 1930.

LEYLAND LINE, LIVERPOOL (1895-1927)

Frederick Leyland & Co Ltd was founded in 1873 as an offshoot of the Bibby Line which operated in the Liverpool-Mediterranean trade. A transatlantic cargo and cattle service was begun three years later.

On 7 September 1895 a passenger service between Liverpool and Boston was established with the sailing of the VICTORIAN, followed three weeks later by her sister ship the ARMENIAN. Six years later a controlling interest in the Atlantic activities of the Line was purchased by the International Mercantile Marine Co, and in subsequent years its ships were freely interchanged among the other members of the group.

World War I resulted in heavy losses to the Company's fleet with the WINNI-FREDIAN emerging as the sole surviving passenger ship. After the war, she resumed her former service, and was joined by the DEVONIAN in 1923.

The number of sailings gradually declined and in the fall of 1927 both ships were transferred to the Red Star Line for a few voyages before being laid up and sold for scrap.

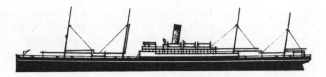

64 WINIFREDIAN
'99, (1899-1929) 10,405. 570 x 59. Single screw, triple expansion engines, 14 knots. Built by Harland & Wolff, Belfast. M.V. Liverpool-Boston, 22 July 1899. Served as troopship 1914-19. Transferred to Red Star Line's Antwerp-New York service for a few voyages 1927. Broken up Italy 1929.

65 DEVONIAN (II)
'02, (1923-29) 13,507. 602 x 60. Twin screw, triple expansion engines, 15 knots. Built by Hawthorn, Leslie & Co, Hebburn-on-Tyne as HANOVERIAN. M.V. Liverpool-Boston, 19 July 1902. Transferred to Dominion Line 1903; renamed MAYFLOWER. Transferred to White Star Line later in the same year; renamed CRETIC. Served as troopship 1915-19. Returned to Leyland Line 1923; renamed DEVONIAN. Transferred to Red Star Line's Antwerp-New York service 1927. Broken up Bo'ness 1929.

CANADIAN PACIFIC, LONDON (1903-   )

The Canadian Pacific Railway Co completed its transcontinental line from Montreal to Vancouver in 1887 and two years later was awarded a mail contract across the Pacific. The next logical step was to establish a transatlantic service to complete the route from Europe to the Far East. In 1903 the Company purchased the Canadian interests of Elder Dempster & Co, including fifteen ships which were continued in operation to provide an emigrant service from European ports to Quebec and Montreal in the summer, shifting to St John, N.B. in the winter months.

Orders were placed for two new express liners, the EMPRESS OF BRITAIN and EMPRESS OF IRELAND. The latter was the victim of a major disaster when, in May 1914, she was involved in a collision during a dense fog in the St Lawrence and sank with a loss of over 1,000 lives. Two additional ships, the MISSANABIE and METAGAMA joined the fleet soon after the start of World War I.

In 1917 the Company took over the Allan Line, its chief competitor in the Canadian trade. The Allan fleet consisted of fifteen ships, including the 18,000 ton liners ALSATIAN and CALGARIAN, and brought the combined fleet to nearly 400,000 tons.

World War I resulted in the loss of eight ships by enemy action, including the MISSANABIE and CALGARIAN, while during the same period three others were wrecked. As a result, the post-war years saw a great expansion of the fleet, including the addition of four ex-German liners, and culminating in the 42,000 ton EMPRESS OF BRITAIN , by far the largest ship yet built for the Canadian trade. This new construction came at an unfortunate time, since the trade slump of the 1930s necessitated the reduction of the fleet to nine ships by 1935.

The Canadian Pacific again provided valuable services in World War II with resultant heavy losses: only three ships survived to return to service. One of these, the EMPRESS OF CANADA, was destroyed by fire in 1953 and was replaced by the purchase of the French Line's DE GRASSE which was renamed EMPRESS OF AUSTRALIA.

Three new ships were built between 1956 and 1961 but, as trade decreased, two were eventually sold. The Line's sole remaining passenger liner the second EMPRESS OF CANADA now carries on the transatlantic service alone.

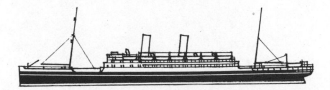

66 MONTROYAL

'06,(1906-30) 15,646. 570 x 65. Twin screw, quadruple expansion engines, 18 knots. Built by Fairfield Shipbuilding & Engineering Co, Govan, Glasgow, as EMPRESS OF BRITAIN; the first "Empress" on the Atlantic. M.V. Liverpool-Quebec, 5 May 1906. Collided with, and sank steamer HELVETIA in fog off Cape Magdeleine, 27 July 1912. Commissioned as armed merchant cruiser August 1914. Served as troopship 1915-19. Resumed passenger service, March 1919. Renamed MONTROYAL 1924. Broken up Stavanger, Norway 1930.

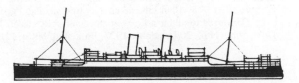

67 METAGAMA

'15,(1915-34) 12,420. 520 x 64. Twin screw, quadruple expansion engines, 16 knots. Built by Barclay, Curle & Co, Glasgow. M.V. Liverpool-St. John, N.B., 26 March 1915. Served as troopship during the war; resumed passenger service, November 1918. Laid up at Southend 1931; broken up Bo'ness 1934.

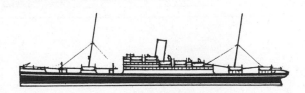

68 MARBURN

'00,(1917-28) 10,576. 518 x 59. Twin screw, triple expansion engines, 16 knots. Built by Alexander Stephen & Sons, Linthouse, Glasgow, as TUNISIAN for Allan Line (Great Britain). Allan Line taken over by Canadian Pacific 1917. Resumed passenger service after war, September 1919. Renamed MARBURN 1922. F.V. Liverpool-St. John, N.B., 17 November 1922. Broken up Genoa 1928.

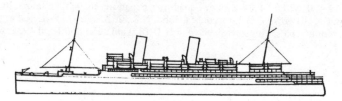

69 MARLOCH

'05, (1917-29) 10,687. 540 x 60. Triple screw, turbines, 15 knots. Built by Workman Clark & Co, Belfast, as VICTORIAN for Allan Line. The first turbine liner built for the North Atlantic service. Served as armed merchant cruiser 1914-18. Allan Line taken over by Canadian Pacific 1917. On Indian trooping service 1921. Converted to oil-burning, re-engined and refitted 1922; renamed MARLOCH. F.V. Glasgow-St. John, N.B., 20 December 1922. Broken up Milford Haven 1929.

70 EMPRESS OF FRANCE (I)

'14, (1919-28) (1929-34) 18,481. 600 x 72. Quadruple screw, turbines, 19 knots. Built by Wm Beardmore & Co, Glasgow, as ALSATIAN for Allan Line (Great Britain). First Atlantic liner with a cruiser stern. Commissioned as armed merchant cruiser in the 10th Cruiser Squadron, August 1914. Allan Line taken over by Canadian Pacific 1917. Refitted at Glasgow 1919; renamed EMPRESS OF FRANCE. F.V. Liverpool-Quebec, 14 November 1919. Transferred to transpacific service for a year, December 1928. Laid up on the Clyde, October 1931; broken up Dalmuir 1934.

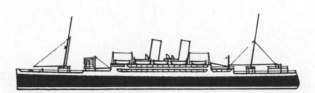

71 MELITA
'18, (1918-35) 15,183. 546 x 67. Triple screw, combination triple expansion engines and turbine, 16 knots. Laid down 1914 by Barclay, Curle & Co, Glasgow, for Hamburg American Line. Work discontinued for duration of war. Hull towed to Belfast for completion by Harland & Wolff as troopship for Canadian Pacific service. M.V. Liverpool-Quebec, 25 January 1918. Sold to Italian shipbreakers and towed to Genoa 1935. Bought by Italian Government for service as troopship; renamed LIGURIA. Set afire by air attack and scuttled at Tobruk, Libya, 22 January 1941. Salvaged 1950; towed to Savona and broken up.

72 MINNEDOSA
'18, (1918-35) 15,186. Details as (71). Laid down 1914 by Barclay, Curle & Co, for Hamburg American Line. Completed by Harland & Wolff 1918. M.V. Liverpool-St. John, N.B., 6 December 1918. Sold to Italian shipbreakers and towed to Savona 1935. Bought by Italian Government for service as troopship; renamed PIEMONTE. Scuttled at Messina, 15 August 1943. Salvaged 1949; towed to La Spezia and broken up.

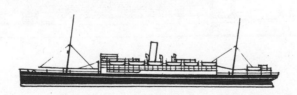

73 MONTREAL (II)
'06, (1921-28) 9,720. 498 x 55. Twin screw, quadruple expansion engines, 15 knots. Built by Blohm & Voss, Hamburg, as KONIG FRIEDRICH AUGUST for Hamburg American Line. Allocated to British Government as reparation 1919. Bought by Canadian Pacific 1920; renamed MONTREAL 1921. F.V. Antwerp-Montreal, 1 June 1921. Laid up at Southend, May 1927. Sold to Fabre Line 1928; renamed ALESIA (205).

43

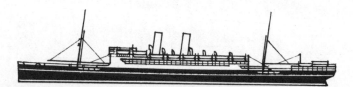

74 MONTNAIRN
'08, (1921-29) 16,992. 613 x 68. Twin screw, quadruple expansion engines, 17 knots. Built by
J.C. Tecklenborg, Geestemunde, as PRINZ FRIEDRICH WILHELM for Norddeutscher Lloyd.
Allocated to British Government as war reparation 1919. Bought by Canadian Pacific 1921;
renamed EMPRESS OF CHINA. Renamed EMPRESS OF INDIA before completion of refit for
passenger service. F.V. Liverpool-Quebec, 23 June 1922. Renamed MONTLAURIER November
same year. Damaged by fire 15 April 1925 while undergoing repairs at Birkenhead; renamed
MONTEITH upon completion. Renamed MONTNAIRN three months later. Laid up at Southend
1929; broken up Genoa 1930.

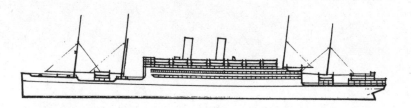

75 EMPRESS OF SCOTLAND (I)
'06, (1922-30) 25,037.699 x 77. Twin screw, quadruple expansion engines, 18 knots. Built by
A.G. Vulkan Werke, Stettin, as KAISERIN AUGUSTE VICTORIA for Hamburg American Line;
the largest ship in the world with passenger accommodations considered to be the most luxurious
afloat. Allocated to British Government as reparation 1919. Served as troopship 1919-20. Bought
by Canadian Pacific 1921; renamed EMPRESS OF SCOTLAND. F.V. Hamburg-Quebec, 14 June
1922. Broken up Blyth 1930.

44

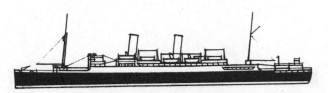

76 MONTCALM (III)
'21, (1922-42) 16,418. 577 x 70. Twin screw, turbines, 16 knots. Built by John Brown & Co,
Clydebank, Glasgow. M.V. Liverpool-St. John, N.B., 17 January 1922. Commissioned as armed
merchant cruiser H M S WOLFE, October 1939. Sold to British Admiralty 1942. Converted to
destroyer depot ship 1946. Laid up in reserve 1950; broken up Faslane 1952.

77 MONTROSE (II)
'22, (1922-40) 16,402. Details as (76). Built by Fairfield Shipbuilding & Engineering Co, Glasgow.
F.V. Liverpool-Montreal, 5 May 1922. Commissioned as armed merchant cruiser H M S FORFAR,
September 1939. Torpedoed and sunk off west coast of Ireland, 2 December 1940.

78 MONTCLARE
'22, (1922-42) 16,314. Details as (76). Built by John Brown & Co. M.V. Liverpool-Montreal,
18 August, 1922. Commissioned as armed merchant cruiser, August 1939. Sold to British Admiralty
1942. Converted to submarine depot ship 1946. Laid up in reserve 1954; broken up Inverkeithing
1958.

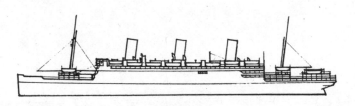

79 EMPRESS OF AUSTRALIA (I)
'19, (1927-39) 21,833. 615 x 75. Twin screw, turbines, 22 knots. Launched December 1913 by
A.G. Vulkan Werke, Stettin, as TIRPITZ for Hamburg American Line; work delayed by war.
Allocated to British Government as reparation 1919. Bought by Canadian Pacific 1921. Refitted
and renamed EMPRESS OF AUSTRALIA 1922; placed on transpacific service. Figured
prominently in relief work at Yokohama during earthquake of September 1923. Refitted 1926
and transferred to transatlantic service; F.V. Southampton-Quebec, 25 June 1927. Converted to
troopship 1939; broken up Inverkeithing 1952.

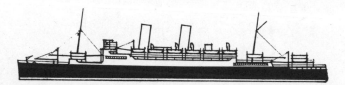

80 DUCHESS OF BEDFORD
'28, (1928-48) 20,123. 601 x 75. Twin screw, turbines, 18 knots. Built by John Brown & Co, Clydebank, Glasgow. M.V. Liverpool-Montreal, 1 June 1928. Converted to troopship 1939. Refitted at Glasgow 1947; renamed EMPRESS OF FRANCE (86) 1948.

81 DUCHESS OF ATHOL
'28, (1928-42) 20,119. Details as (80). Built by Wm. Beardmore & Co, Glasgow. M.V. Liverpool-Montreal, 13 July 1928. Converted to troopship 1939. Torpedoed and sunk in South Atlantic, 10 October 1942.

82 DUCHESS OF RICHMOND
'29, (1929-47) 20,022. Details as (80). Built by John Brown & Co. M.V. Liverpool-St John, N.B., 15 March 1929. Converted to troopship 1940. Refitted 1946; renamed EMPRESS OF CANADA (85) 1947.

83 DUCHESS OF YORK
'29, (1929-43) 20,021. Details as (80). Built by John Brown & Co. M. V. Liverpool-St John, N.B. 22 March 1929. Converted to troopship 1940. Sunk by German bombers off Cape St Vincent, 11 July 1943.

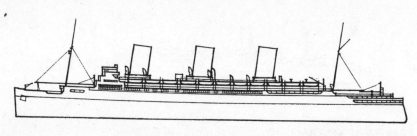

84 EMPRESS OF BRITAIN (II)
'31, (1931-40) 42,348. 761 x 98. Quadruple screw, turbines, 24 knots. Built by John Brown & Co M.V. Southampton-Quebec, 27 May 1931. Largest and most luxurious ship ever built for the St Lawrence service. Engaged in round-the-world cruising during winter months. Converted to troopship 1939. Attacked by enemy aircraft and set afire 70 miles northwest of Ireland, 26 October 1940. Torpedoed and sunk while under tow by Polish destroyer BURZA two days later.

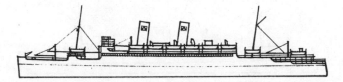

85 EMPRESS OF CANADA (I)
'29, (1947-53) 20,022. Formerly DUCHESS OF RICHMOND (82). Refitted after war service 1947;
renamed EMPRESS OF CANADA. F.V. Liverpool-Montreal, 16 July 1947. Caught fire 25 January
1953 at Gladstone Dock, Liverpool and became a total loss. Hulk refloated and towed to Italy;
broken up La Spezia 1954.

86 EMPRESS OF FRANCE (II)
'28, (1948-60) 20,448. Formerly DUCHESS OF BEDFORD (80). Refitted 1947; renamed
EMPRESS OF FRANCE 1948. F.V. Liverpool-Montreal, 1 September 1948. Broken up Newport
1960.

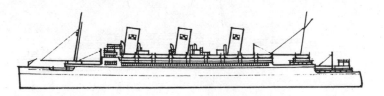

87 EMPRESS OF SCOTLAND (II)
'30, (1950-57) 26,313. 616 x 83. Twin screw, turbines, 20 knots. Built by Fairfield Shipbuilding
& Engineering Co, Govan, Glasgow, as EMPRESS OF JAPAN. On transpacific service 1930-39.
Converted to troopship 1939. Renamed EMPRESS OF SCOTLAND 1942 after Japanese entry
into war. Refitted for Atlantic service 1948; F.V. Liverpool-Quebec, 9 May 1950. Sold to Hamburg
Atlantic Line 1958; renamed HANSEATIC (182).

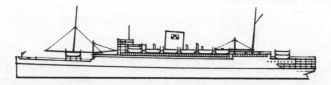

88 EMPRESS OF AUSTRALIA (II)

'24, (1953-56) 19,918. Formerly DE GRASSE (193) Cie. Generale Transatlantique. Bought by Canadian Pacific as replacement for EMPRESS OF CANADA 1953; renamed EMPRESS OF AUSTRALIA. F.V. Liverpool-Montreal, 28 April 1953. Sold to Grimaldi-Siosa Line 1956; renamed VENEZUELA. Ran aground and beached near Cannes, 17 March 1962; broken up La Spezia .

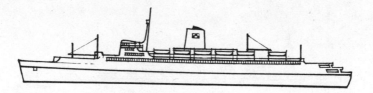

89 EMPRESS OF BRITAIN (III)

'56, (1956-64) 25,516. 640 x 85. Twin screw, turbines, 20 knots. Built by Fairfield Shipbuilding & Engineering Co, Govan, Glasgow. M.V. Liverpool-Montreal, 20 April 1956. Sold to Greek Line, November 1964; renamed QUEEN ANNA MARIA (232).

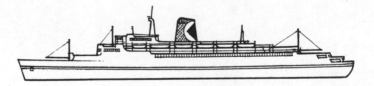

90 EMPRESS OF ENGLAND
'57, (1957-70) 24,467. Details as (89). Built by Vickers-Armstrongs, Walker-on-Tyne. M.V.
Liverpool-Montreal, 18 April 1957. Sold to Shaw Savill Line (Great Britain) for cruising service,
1970; renamed OCEAN MONARCH.

91 EMPRESS OF CANADA (II) ●
'61, (1961-) 25,615. 650 x 87. Twin screw, turbines, 21 knots. Built by Vickers-Armstrongs,
M.V. Liverpool-Montreal, 24 April 1961.

DONALDSON LINE, GLASGOW (1905-1966)

Established in 1855 by the Donaldson brothers of Glasgow to develop trade between the Clyde and South American ports, the service was transferred to Canada in 1876 and, as a result of the heavy Scottish migration to Canada at the turn of the century, a passenger service from glasgow to St John, N.B., Quebec and Montreal was begun with the sailing of the ATHENIA on 25 March 1905. In the following years the Company added the CASSANDRA and the sister ships SATURNIA and LETITIA. All four ships were engaged in Government service during the first World War, during which the ATHENIA was torpedoed and the LETITIA wrecked near Halifax. They were replaced by a second ATHENIA and LETITIA in 1923-25, thus enabling the SATURNIA to be withdrawn and CASSANDRA to be converted to a cargo ship.

In World War II, the second ATHENIA was also torpedoed and in 1946 the LETITIA was sold to the British Government. To keep the service alive two American "Victory" ships were purchased and fitted with limited passenger accommodations and, in October 1948, the LISMORIA sailed from Glasgow, followed a few months later by the LAURENTIA. Sailings were discontinued at the end of 1966 and, the following year, the two ships were broken up and the remainder of the fleet sold, marking the end of a company which had existed for 112 years.

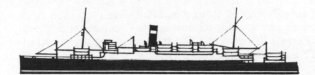

92 ATHENIA (II)
'23, (1923-39) 13,465. 538 x 66. Twin screw, turbines, 15 knots. Built by Fairfield Shipbuilding
& Engineering Co, Govan, Glasgow. M.V. Glasgow-Montreal, 21 April 1923. Torpedoed and sunk
by German submarine U-30, 200 miles west of the Hebrides, with a loss of 112 lives, 3 September
1939; the first passenger ship sunk in World War II.

93 LETITIA (II)
'25, (1925-46) 13,475. Details as (92). Built by Fairfield Shipbuilding & Engineering Co. M.V.
Glasgow-Montreal, 24 April 1925. Commissioned as armed merchant cruiser 1939; later served
as troopship. Taken over by Canadian Government and converted to hospital ship 1944. Sold to
British Ministry of Transport 1946; renamed EMPIRE BRENT. Served as troopship to Far East
and on Australian emigration service 1948-50. Chartered to New Zealand Government and refitted
as emigrant ship under Donaldson management 1951; renamed CAPTAIN COOK. Chartered by
Donaldson Line for a number of transatlantic voyages in summer of 1955. Broken up Inverkeithing
1960.

FURNESS WARREN LINE, LIVERPOOL (1913-1961)

In 1865, George Warren & Co established a line of screw steamers to carry steerage passengers between Liverpool, Boston and Philadelphia, and in 1912, Furness, Withey & Co Ltd acquired a controlling interest in the Company which eventually became known as the Furness Warren Line. The following year the 4,000 ton Furness steamer DIGBY entered the Liverpool-St John, N.B. and Halifax service and was joined by the SACHEM, a cargo vessel fitted to carry passengers.

Two sister ships, the NEWFOUNDLAND and NOVA SCOTIA, completed in 1925-26 were lost in World War II. They were replaced by a second pair which revived their names. However, adverse trade conditions resulted in their accommodation being reduced to 12 berths in 1961 and a year later they were sold to end the Line's services.

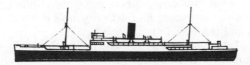

94 NEWFOUNDLAND (I)
'25, (1925-43) 6,791. 423 x 55. Twin screw, quadruple expansion engines, 15 knots. 185 passengers. Built by Vickers-Armstrongs, Barrow-in-Furness. M.V. Liverpool-Boston, January 1925. Converted to hospital ship at outbreak of World War II. Bombed and sunk off Salerno, 13 September 1943.

95 NOVA SCOTIA (I)
'26, (1926-42) 6,796. Details as (94). Built by Vickers-Armstrongs. M.V. Liverpool Boston, 25 May 1926. Converted for duty as troopship. Torpedoed and sunk off Laurenco Marques, Mozambique, with the loss of over 500 lives while transporting Italian prisoners of war, 4 December 1942.

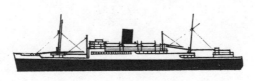

96 NOVA SCOTIA (II)
'47, (1947-61) 7,438. 441 x 61. Single screw, turbines, 16 knots. 160 passengers. Built by Vickers-Armstrongs. M.V. Liverpool-Boston, 2 September 1947. Reduced to 12 passengers 1961. Sold to Dominion Far East Line (Great Britain) 1962; renamed FRANCIS DRAKE. Placed on Japan-Australia service. Broken up Kaohsiung, Taiwan 1971.

97 NEWFOUNDLAND (II)
'48, (1948-61) 7,437. Details as (96). Built by Vickers-Armstrongs. M.V. Liverpool-Boston, 14 February 1948. Reduced to 12 passengers 1961. Sold to Dominion Far East Line 1962; renamed GEORGE ANSON. Broken up Kaohsiung, 1971.

ROYAL MAIL, LONDON (1921-27)

The Royal Mail Steam Packet Co, one of the oldest British steamship companies, was chartered in 1839 for carrying mail from Great Britain to the West Indies. Service began in 1841 with a fleet of fourteen steamers and three sailing vessels. Over the years a long line of famous ships sailed on the Company's traditional services to Brazil, the River Plate and the West Indies.

The R.M.S.P. entered the North Atlantic trade in 1921, running from Hamburg to New York via Southampton with three ships acquired from the Pacific Steam Navigation Co. These were later supplemented by the converted cargo ship ORCA and by the former German liner MUNCHEN which was renamed OHIO. The OROPESA one of the original trio, was then returned to the P.S.N. South American service.

Due to immigration restrictions and adverse trade conditions, the venture was not as successful as anticipated and the service was discontinued in 1927. The OHIO and ORCA were transferred to the White Star fleet, while the ORBITA and ORDUNA were returned to their previous owners.

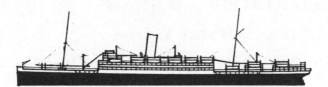

98 ORBITA
'15, (1921-27) 15,486. 569 x 67. Triple screw, combination triple expansion engines and turbine,
15 knots. Built by Harland & Wolff, Belfast, for Pacific Steam Navigation Co (Great Britain) for
service to west coast of South America. Transferred to Royal Mail for transatlantic service; F.V.
Hamburg-New York, 30 April 1921. Returned to Pacific Steam Navigation Co 1927. Broken up
Newport 1950.

99 ORDUNA
'14, (1921-27) 15,499. Details as (98). Built by Harland & Wolff for Pacific Steam Navigation Co.
Chartered to Cunard Line 1914-19. Transferred to Royal Mail; F.V. Hamburg-New York, 28 May
1921. Returned to Pacific Steam Navigation Co 1927. Broken up Dalmuir 1951.

100 ORCA
'18, (1923-27) 16,063. 574 x 67. Triple screw, combination triple expansion engines and turbine,
15 knots. Built by Harland & Wolff as cargo ship for Pacific Steam Navigation Co. Passenger
accommodations added 1922. Transferred to Royal Mail 1923; F.V. Hamburg-New York, 3
January 1923. Transferred to White Star Line 1927; renamed CALGARIC (49).

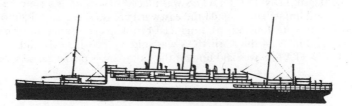

101 OHIO
'23, (1923-27) 18,940. 614 x 72. Twin screw, quadruple expansion engines, 17 knots. Laid down
by A.G. Weser, Bremen as MUNCHEN for Norddeutscher Lloyd. Ceded to Great Britain as war
reparation while still under construction 1919. Acquired by Royal Mail 1920; renamed OHIO.
Completion delayed for three years; M.V. Hamburg-New York, 4 April 1923. Transferred to
White Star Line 1927; renamed ALBERTIC (48).

2 UNITED STATES

UNITED STATES LINES, NEW YORK (1921-69)

At the end of World War I, the United States Shipping Board turned over a large fleet of ex-German liners and war-built troopships to the United States Mail Steamship Co to operate a transatlantic service. The enterprise was a complete failure and it became necessary for the Shipping Board to take over the Company in 1921 under the name of the United States Lines. The fleet consisted of fifteen ships, including the former German liners GEORGE WASHINGTON, AMERICA and LEVIATHAN. The following year two ex-German ships, the POTOMAC and SUSQUEHANNA, were withdrawn from service, and in 1924 seven ships were sold, including five ex-troopships of the "502" class, to the Dollar Line.

The operations of the Shipping Board continued to show a financial deficit, and in 1929 the six ships of the fleet, plus five ships of the American Merchant Lines, were sold to P.W. Chapman & Co. However, the Chapman Company failed to carry out the terms of the agreement and in October 1931 were foreclosed by the Shipping Board. The GEORGE WASHINGTON, AMERICA and REPUBLIC were withdrawn from service and the three remaining ships, plus the AMERICAN IMPORTER and AMERICAN TRAVELLER, were sold to the International Mercantile Marine Co. At the same time, the American Merchant Line's ships were added to the fleet.

In 1932-33, two new ships, the MANHATTEN and WASHINGTON were commissioned and as a result, the LEVIATHAN was laid up soon afterward. World War II brought a suspension of the Line's sailings and in 1940 the PRESIDENT HARDING as well as the seven ships of the AMERICAN MERCHANT class were sold to a newly formed Belgian flag subsidiary. All except one were sunk by enemy action.

The AMERICA (II) was completed in 1940 only to be converted soon afterward to serve as a Navy transport. In the post-war shortage of tonnage between 1946 and 1949, eight C-4 type transports of the "MARINE" class were chartered from the U.S. Maritime Commission to operate a one-class service with dormitory accommodations.

In 1952 the flagship UNITED STATES was placed in service as a running mate of the AMERICA and immediately made the eastward crossing at a speed almost four knots faster than the previous record. Financial problems continued to plague the Line however, and in 1964 the AMERICA was sold to the Chandris Lines. Five years later the UNITED STATES was laid up and the Company's passenger service came to an end.

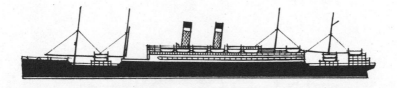

102 AMERICA (I)
'05, (1921-31) 22,625. 687 x 74. Twin-screw, quadruple expansion engines, 18 knots. Built by
Harland & Wolff, Belfast, as AMERIKA for Hamburg American Line. M.V. Hamburg - New York, 11
October 1905. Interned at Boston 1914. Seized by United States Government for service as troop-
ship 1917; renamed AMERICA. Refitted and chartered to United States Mail Steamship Co, 1921.
F.V. New York-Bremen, 22 June 1921; transferred to United States Lines later in year. Laid up in
Patuxent River, Maryland 1931. Converted to Army transport 1941; renamed EDMUND B.
ALEXANDER. Laid up at Baltimore 1948; broken up 1957.

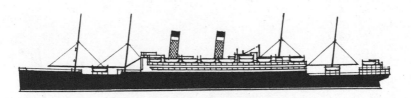

103 GEORGE WASHINGTON
'09, (1921-31) 25,507. 722 x 78. Twin-screw, quadruple expansion engines, 18 knots. Built by
Vulkan A.G.,Stettin, for Norddeutscher Lloyd. M.V. Bremen - New York, 12 June 1909. Interned
at New York 1914. Seized by United States Government as troopship 1917. Carried President
Wilson to the Versailles Conference 1919. Refitted and chartered to United States Mail Steamship
Co 1921. F.V. New York-Bremen, 3 August 1921; transferred to United States Lines after one
voyage. Laid up in Patuxent River 1931. Converted to Army transport 1943. Laid up at Baltimore
1947; gutted by fire, 17 January 1951 and broken up.

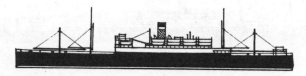

104   PRESIDENT ROOSEVELT
'22, (1922-40) 14,127. 535 x 72. Twin screw, turbines, 18 knots. Built by New York Shipbuilding
Corp., Camden, New Jersey, as "535" class troopship PENINSULA STATE for U.S. Shipping
Board. M.V. New York-Bremen, February 1922. Renamed PRESIDENT PIERCE, May 1922;
renamed PRESIDENT ROOSEVELT three months later. Rescued crew of British cargo ship
ANTINOE in mid-Atlantic gale, January 1926. Commissioned as U.S. Navy transport 1941;
renamed U S S JOSEPH T. DICKMAN (AP-26) Laid up at Suisun Bay, California, March 1946;
broken up 1948.

105   PRESIDENT HARDING
'22, (1922-40) 14,127. Details as (104). Built by New York Shipbuilding Corp. as LONE STAR
STATE for U.S. Shipping Board. M.V. New York-Bremen, March 1922. Renamed PRESIDENT
TAFT 1922; renamed PRESIDENT HARDING 1922. Sold to Antwerp Navigation Co (Belgium)
1940; renamed VILLE DE BRUGES. Bombed and sunk in River Scheldt, 14 May 1940.

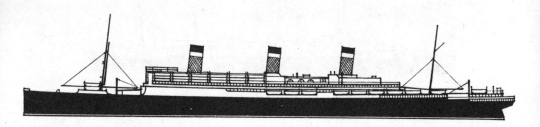

106   LEVIATHAN
'14, (1923-37) 54,282. 950 x 100. Quadruple screw, turbines, 23 knots. Built by Blohm & Voss,
Hamburg, as VATERLAND for Hamburg American Line. M.V. Hamburg-New York, 14 May 1914
Interned at New York 1914. Seized by United States Government for service as troopship 1917;
renamed LEVIATHAN. Acquired by United States Lines and refitted at Newport News, Virginia,
1923. F.V. New York-Southampton, 4 July 1923. Laid up at New York 1934; sailed to Rosyth,
Scotland for breaking up 1938.

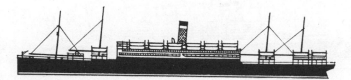

107 REPUBLIC

'07, (1924-31) 17,910. 615 x 68. Twin screw, quadruple expansion engines, 14 knots. Launched 1903 by Harland & Wolff, Belfast, as SCOTIAN for Wilson's & Furness-Leyland Line (Great Britain). Purchased during construction by Hamburg American Line; renamed PRESIDENT GRANT. M.V. Hamburg-New York, 14 September 1907. Interned in New York 1914; requisitioned by United States Government as troopship 1917. Assigned to United States Lines 1924; renamed REPUBLIC. F.V. Hamburg-New York, 29 April 1924. Laid up 1931. Served as U.S. Navy transport in World War II. Broken up Baltimore 1952.

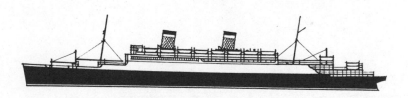

108 MANHATTAN

'32, (1932-41) 24,289. 705 x 86. Twin screw, turbines, 21 knots. Built by New York Shipbuilding Corp., Camden, New Jersey. M.V. New York-Hamburg, 10 August 1932. Commissioned as U.S. Navy transport 1941; renamed U S S WAKEFIELD (AP-21). Caught fire while in convoy, 3 September 1942. Passengers and crew abandoned ship; brought into Halifax by salvage crew. Returned to Navy service April 1944. Laid up in Hudson River reserve fleet 1946; broken up Kearny, New Jersey 1965.

109 WASHINGTON

'33, (1933-51) 24,627. Details as (108). Built by New York Shipbuilding Corp. M.V. New York-Hamburg, 10 May 1933. Commissioned as U.S. Navy transport 1941; renamed U S S MOUNT VERNON (AP-22). Resumed passenger service Feburary 1948; renamed WASHINGTON. Returned to Military Sea Transportation Service, October 1951. Laid up in Hudson River reserve fleet February 1953; broken up Kearny 1964.

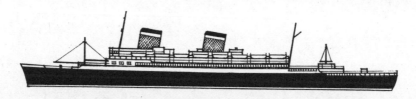

110 AMERICA (II)

'40, (1946-64) 33,961. 723 x 93. Twin screw, turbines, 23 knots. Built by Newport News Ship-building & Drydock Co, Newport News, Virginia. M.V. New York-West Indies, 10 August 1940. Commissioned as U.S. Navy transport 1942; renamed U S S WEST POINT (AP-23). Refitted at Newport News 1946; renamed AMERICA. F.V. New York-Le Havre, 14 November 1946. Sold to Chandris Lines 1964; renamed AUSTRALIS.

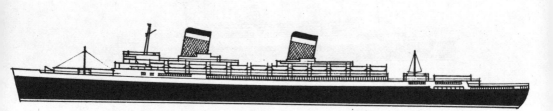

111 UNITED STATES

'52, (1952-69) 53,329. 990 x 101. Quadruple screw, turbines, 33 knots. Built by Newport News Shipbuilding & Drydock Co. The largest passenger ship built in the United States. M.V. New York-Southampton, 3 July 1952. Won the "Blue Riband", breaking by a wide margin the transatlantic speed record previously held by the QUEEN MARY by making the eastbound crossing at an average speed of 35.59 knots. Existing record also broken on return westward passage. Laid up at Newport News, November 1969.

AMERICAN EXPORT ISBRANDTSEN LINES, NEW YORK (1931-69)

The American Export Line began its passenger services between New York and the Mediterranean in 1931 when the "Four Aces", the EXCALIBUR, EXOCHORDA, EXETER and EXCAMBION, were placed in service. In 1940-41 all four ships were commissioned as U.S. Navy transports and three were sunk by enemy action during the course of the war. The sole survivor, the EXOCHORDA, was sold to the Turkish Maritime Lines.

As replacements, the Line purchased four Navy attack transports in 1947 and converted them for passenger service, reviving the names of the earlier quartet. Orders were placed for two large liners and the transport GENERAL W.P. RICHARDSON was chartered, refitted and renamed LA GUARDIA. Upon completion of the new ships, INDEPENDENCE and CONSTITUTION in 1951, the LA GUARDIA was withdrawn from service and seven years later the American Banner Line's ATLANTIC was added to the fleet.

In 1960, two of the "Four Aces" were laid up, followed by the sale of the second pair five years later. Rising operating costs caused the withdrawal from service of the Company's three remaining passenger liners in 1968-69.

112 EXCALIBUR (I)
'31, (1931-41) 9,359. 474 x 61. Single screw, turbines, 16 knots. Built by New York Shipbuilding
Corp., Camden, New Jersey. M.V. New York-Mediterranean 1931. Commissioned as U.S. Navy
transport 1941; renamed U S S JOSEPH HEWES (AP-50). Torpedoed and sunk off Casablanca,
11 November 1942.

113 EXOCHORDA (I)
'31, (1931-41) 9,360. Details as (112). Built by New York Shipbuilding Corp. M.V. New York-
Mediterranean 1931. Commissioned as U.S. Navy transport 1940; renamed U S S HARRY LEE
(APA-10). Sold to Turkish Maritime Lines (Turkey) 1946; renamed TARSUS. Gutted by fire
following collision with Yugoslav tanker PETAR ZORANIC in Bosphorus, 14 December 1960.

114 EXETER (I)
'31, (1931-41 9,360. Details as (112) Built by New York Shipbuilding Corp. M.V. New York-
Mediterranean 1931. Commissioned as U.S. Navy transport 1941; renamed U S S EDWARD
RUTLEDGE (AP-52). Torpedoed and sunk off Casablanca, 12 November 1942.

115 EXCAMBION (I)
'31, (1931-41) 9,359. Details as (112). Built by New York Shipbuilding Corp. M.V. New York-
Mediterranean 1931. Commissioned as U.S. Navy transport 1941; renamed U S S JOHN PENN
(AP-51). Sunk by Japanese planes off Guadalcanal, 13 August 1943.

116 EXOCHORDA (II)
'44, (1948-60) 9,644. 473 x 66. Single screw, turbines, 18 knots. Built by Bethlehem Steel Corp.,
Sparrows Point, Maryland, as U.S. Navy attack transport U S S DAUPHIN (APA-97). Bought by
American Export Line and refitted to carry 125 passengers, 1948; renamed EXOCHORDA.
F.V. New York-Mediterranean, 2 November 1948. Laid up in reserve fleet 1960. Converted to
floating dormitory, Stevens Institute of Technology, Hoboken, New Jersey, 1967.

117 EXCAMBION (II)
'44, (1948-60) 9,644. Details as (116). Built by Bethlehem Steel Corp. as U S S QUEENS (APA-103).
Bought by American Export Lines 1948; renamed EXCAMBION. F.V. New York-Mediterranean,
3 December 1948. Laid up in reserve fleet 1960. Sold to State of Texas as training ship 1965;
renamed TEXAS CLIPPER.

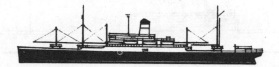

118 EXCALIBUR (II)
'44, (1948-65) 9,644. Details as (116). Built by Bethlehem Steel Corp. as U S S DUTCHESS (APA-98).
Bought by American Export Line 1948; renamed EXCALIBUR. F.V. New York-Mediterranean,
24 September 1948. Sold to Orient Overseas Line (Liberia)1965; renamed ORIENTAL JADE.

119 EXETER (II)
'44, (1948-65) 9,644. Details as (116). Built by Bethlehem Steel Corp. as U S S SHELBY(APA-105).
Bought by American Export Line 1948; renamed EXETER. F.V. New York-Mediterranean,
1 December 1948. Sold to Orient Overseas Line 1965; renamed ORIENTAL PEARL.

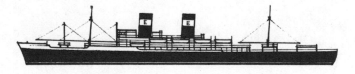

120 LA GUARDIA
'44, (1949-51) 18,298. 622 x 75. Twin screw, turbines, 20 knots. Built by Federal Shipbuilding Co,
Kearny, New Jersey as Type P2 "General" class troopship GENERAL WILDS P. RICHARDSON.
Chartered by American Export Line 1948; reconditioned at Pascagoula, Mississippi and renamed
LA GUARDIA. F.V. New York-Genoa, 27 May 1949. Laid up in James River reserve fleet December
1951. Bought by Hawaiian Steamship Co (United States) for new Californian-Hawaii service 1956;
renamed LEILANI. Laid up at San Francisco, December 1958 and repossessed by U.S. Maritime
Administration. Bought by American President Lines (United States) 1960 and extensively remodelled at Seattle; renamed PRESIDENT ROOSEVELT 1961. Sold to Chandris Lines 1970;
renamed ATLANTIS.

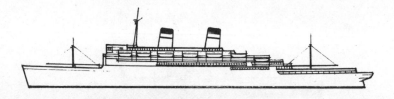

121 INDEPENDENCE
'51, (1951-69) 23,754. 683 x 89. Twin screw, turbines, 22 knots. Built by Bethlehem Steel Co, Quincy, Massachusetts. M.V. New York-Mediterranean ports, 10 February 1951. Laid up at Baltimore 1969.

122 CONSTITUTION
'51, (1951-68) 23,754. Details as (121). Built by Bethlehem Steel Co, Quincy. M.V. New York-Mediterranean ports, 21 June 1951. Laid up at Jacksonville, Florida 1968.

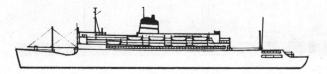

123 ATLANTIC
'53, (1958-68) 14,138. 564 x 76. Single screw, turbines, 20 knots. Built by Sun Shipbuilding & Dry Dock Co, Chester, Pennsylvania as cargo ship BADGER MARINER. Bought by American Banner Lines (United States), a subsidiary of Arnold Bernstein, 1957; renamed ATLANTIC. Refitted as passenger ship at Pascagoula 1958. F.V. New York-Amsterdam, 11 June 1958. Bought by American Export Line 1959. F.V. New York-Haifa, 16 May 1960. Laid up at Baltimore 1968. Sold to Orient Overseas Line 1971; renamed UNIVERSE CAMPUS. Registered in Bahamas.

3 ITALY

NAVIGAZIONE GENERALE ITALIANA, GENOA (1881-1932)

The N.G.I. was formed in 1881 by an amalgamation of two established shipping companies, I. & V. Florio of Palermo, which for four years had been running a service from Palermo to New York, and Raffaele Rubattino of Genoa, whose ships operated primarily to the Far East. The Company's transatlantic service was begun with two Florio steamers, the VINCENZO FLORIO and the WASHINGTON. Four years later the Company entered the South American trade.

In succeeding years the Company acquired three subsidiaries: La Veloce in 1901, Italia in 1906, and Lloyd Italiano in 1907. All four lines retained their identities and provided joint service to both North and South America. In order to concentrate on the transatlantic trade, the ships of the Mediterranean and Far East services were sold in 1910 and in 1917 a new company, Transoceanica, was formed to absorb the Italia Line.

Four N.G.I. ships were lost during World War I and the Line therefore took over the Lloyd Italiano in 1918 and Transoceanica in 1921, while La Veloce was dissolved in 1924. Two new ships, the GIULIO CESARE and DUILIO, which had been ordered before the war, were finally completed in 1922-23 and served to revitalize the fleet which was approaching obsolescence.

Four years later, two additional liners, the ROMA and AUGUSTUS, were commissioned and thus allowed the previous pair to be transferred to the South American service. In 1929 an order was placed for a new 50,000 ton express liner, the REX, but before its completion, the Italian Government ordered the amalgamation of the Company into the "Italia"-Flotte Riunite Cosulich-Lloyd Sabaudo-N.G.I.; the start of the present Italian Line.

124 COLOMBO

'17. (1921-34) 12,087, 536 x 64. Twin screw, quadruple expansion engines, 16 knots. Built by Palmer's Shipbuilding & Iron Co, Jarrow-on-Tyne, as SAN GENNARO for Transoceanica (Italy). Acquired by N.G.I. 1921; renamed COLOMBO. F.V. Genoa-New York, 22 November 1921. Transferred to Lloyd Triestino (Italy) 1934. Scuttled at Massawa, Eritrea, 8 April 1941.

125 GIULIO CESARE

'22, (1922-28) 21,657. 635 x 76. Quadruple screw, turbines, 19 knots. Laid down 1913 by Swan, Hunter & Wigham Richardson, Wallsend-on-Tyne; work suspended during war. M.V. Genoa-Buenos Aires, 4 May 1922; transferred to North Atlantic service three months later. Returned to River Plate service 1928. Transferred to Italian Line 1932; placed in South African service the following year. Transferred to Lloyd Triestino 1935 for Far East service. Converted to troopship 1939. Bombed and sunk at Trieste, 11 September 1944.

126 DUILIO

'23, (1923-28) 24,281. Details as (125). Laid down 1914 by S.A. Ansaldo, Sestri Ponente; work suspended during war. M.V. Genoa-New York, 30 October, 1923. Transferred to South American service 1928. Transferred to Italian Line 1932; placed in South African service the following year. Transferred to Lloyd Triestino 1935. Served as hospital ship in World War II; bombed and sunk at Trieste, 10 July 1944.

LLOYD SABAUDO, GENOA (1907-32)

The Lloyd Sabaudo Societa Anonima di Navigazione was founded in 1906 at Turin, opening its service from Genoa to New York in May of the following year with the sailing of the RE D'ITALIA. In 1908 a service was started to South America.

Upon Italy's entrance into World War I, the German liner MOLTKE was seized by the Italian Government and later sold to the Company which renamed her PESARO and placed her on the post-war North Atlantic service. In 1922-23, two 17,000 ton ships, the CONTE ROSSO and CONTE VERDE, were commissioned, allowing the Line's older vessels to be transferred to the South American service. They, in turn, were replaced on the North Atlantic upon the completion of the still larger CONTE BIANCAMANO and CONTE GRANDE.

In 1931, the Line launched the express liner CONTE DI SAVOIA. However, with the formation of the "Italia"-Flotte Riunite Cosulich-Lloyd Sabaudo-N.G.I. in 1932, the Lloyd Sabaudo ceased to exist and the new ship joined the combined fleet upon completion.

127 CONTE ROSSO

'22, (1922-28) 17,048. 588 x 74. Twin screw, turbines, 18 knots. Built by Wm Beardmore & Co. Glasgow. M.V. Genoa - New York, 19 Febuary 1922. Transferred to South American service 1928. Sold to Lloyd Triestino (Italy) 1932. Converted to troopship 1940. Torpedoed and sunk by British submarine H M S UPHOLDER off Sicily, 24 May 1941.

128 CONTE VERDE

'23, (1923-26) 18,765. Details as (127). Built by Wm Beardmore & Co. M.V. Genoa-New York, 21 April 1923. Transferred to South American service 1926. Sold to Lloyd Triestino 1932. In Shanghai at outbreak of World War II: lay off the Bund until 1942, unable to leave due to British blockade. After Italy's capitulation in 1943, scuttled to avoid capture by Japanese. Refloated and sailed to Japan for conversion to troopship. Sunk by American aircraft, December 1944. Again refloated June 1949 and laid up at Maiguru; broken up 1951.

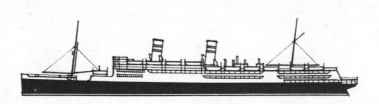

129 CONTE GRANDE

'28, (1928-32) 23,842. 652 x 78. Twin screw, turbines, 19 knots. Built by Stabilimento Tecnico, Trieste. M.V. Genoa - New York, 13 April 1928. Transferred to Italian Line 1932; placed on South American service. Interned at Santos, Brazil, 1941. Bought by United States Government and commissioned as U.S. Navy transport 1942; renamed U S S MONTICELLO (AP-61). Returned to Italian Line, July 1947; renamed CONTE GRANDE. Resumed South American service, July 1949. Transferred to Lloyd Triestino 1960. Broken up La Spezia 1961.

COSULICH LINE, TRIESTE (1920-32)

The Fratelli Cosulich of Trieste founded the Union Austriaca di Navigazione in 1903, inaugurating a passenger service between Trieste and New York the following year. In 1911 the Company's services were extended to South America.

World War I brought a complete halt to the Line's activities and after Trieste came under Italian rule in 1919, the Company was re-established as the Cosulich Societa di Navigazione. The largest of the Company's ships, the KAISER FRANZ JOSEF I, renamed PRESIDENTE WILSON, made the first post-war sailing in 1920.

In 1928 two new 24,000 ton motorships, the SATURNIA and VULCANIA, were added to the North Atlantic service and the older ships were sold. Four years later the Line was incorporated into the "Italia" combination and contributed the SATURNIA and VULCANIA to the joint fleet.

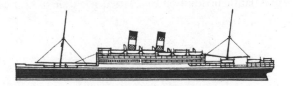

130 PRESIDENTE WILSON
'12, (1920-29) 12,567. 500 x 62. Twin screw, quadruple expansion engines, 18 knots. Built by Cantieri Navale Triestino, Monfalcone, as KAISER FRANZ JOSEF I for Unione Austriaca (Austria). F.V. Trieste - New York, 9 May 1912. Company registered as Cosulich Line when Trieste ceded to Italy after World War I. Renamed GENERALE DIAZ 1919. Resumed passenger service 1920; renamed PRESIDENTE WILSON. Sold to Lloyd Triestino 1929; renamed GANGE and placed on Far East service. Transferred to Adriatica Line (Italy) 1932; renamed MARCO POLO. Scuttled by Germans at La Spezia, 12 May 1944.

ITALIAN LINE, GENOA (1932-)

The "Italia"- Flotte Riunite Cosulich-Lloyd Sabaudo-N.G.I. was formed in 1932 under the direction of the Italian Government, by combining the three leading Italian shipping companies in an effort to eliminate wasteful competition and to increase efficiency through joint management. From the North Atlantic service, the N.G.I. contributed the ROMA and AUGUSTUS, as well as the unfinished REX: from the Lloyd Sabaudo came the CONTE GRANDE, CONTE BIANCAMANO and the incomplete CONTE DI SAVOIA; while the Cosulich Line added the SATURNIA and VULCANIA.

The CONTE GRANDE and CONTE BIANCAMANO were shifted to the South American service when the new express liners REX and CONTE DI SAVOIA entered service in the fall of 1932. After a trouble-plagued maiden voyage, the REX enhanced Italy's maritime prestige the following year by breaking the BREMEN'S speed record for the west bound crossing.

The Italian Line fleet was badly battered in World War II which resulted in the sinking of the four largest ships, the REX, CONTE DI SAVOIA, ROMA and AUGUSTUS. The only survivors, ships which had been seized for war service under the American flag, were returned to Italian control after the war and the VULCANIA and SATURNIA resumed the Line's transatlantic service in 1947.

In 1953-54, two new ships, the ANDREA DORIA and the CRISTOFORO COLOMBO were commissioned to augment the fleet. However, in July 1956, the beautiful new ANDREA DORIA collided with the Swedish American liner STOCKHOLM off Nantucket and sank. She was replaced in 1960 by the LEONARDO DA VINCI and five years later, the sister ships MICHELANGELO and RAFFAELLO were commissioned. This allowed the disposal of the SATURNIA and VULCANIA after nearly forty years of service.

Today, four modern liners of the Italian Line provide the most extensive express service on the North Atlantic in addition to a varied schedule of cruises.

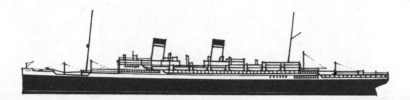

131 ROMA

'26, (1926-41) 32,583. 709 x 83. Quadruple screw, turbines, 21 knots. Built by S.A. Ansaldo, Sestri Ponente, for Navigazione Generale Italiana. M.V. Genoa - New York, 21 September 1926. Transferred to Italian Line 1932. Requisitioned by Italian Navy 1941 for conversion to aircraft carrier; renamed AQUILA. Damaged by British air attacks 1944-45. Sunk by Italian guided torpedoes at Genoa, 19 April 1945, to prevent scuttling by Germans at harbour entrance; refloated and broken up La Spezia 1950.

132 AUGUSTUS (I)

'27, (1928-43) 30,418. 710 x 83. Quadruple screw, motorship, 19 knots. Built by S.A. Ansaldo for N.G.I.; placed on South American service. F.V. Genoa - New York, 28 August 1928. Transferred to Italian Line 1932. Taken over by Italian Navy for conversion to aircraft carrier 1943; renamed SPARVIERO. Scuttled by Germans as block-ship at Genoa, September 1944; refloated and broken up 1947.

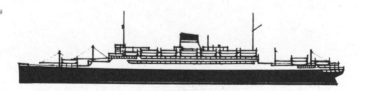

133 SATURNIA

'27, (1928-65) 23,346. 631 x 79. Twin screw, motorship, 19 knots. Built by Cantieri Navale Triestino, Monfalcone, for Cosulich Line. Placed on South American service. F.V. Trieste-New York, 1 February 1928. Transferred to Italian Line 1932. Seized by United States forces and converted to hospital ship 1944; renamed FRANCES Y. SLANGER. Returned to Italian Line, 1946; renamed SATURNIA. Resumed passenger service August 1947. Laid up at Trieste, April 1965; broken up La Spezia.

134 VULCANIA

'28, (1928-65) 24,496. Details as (133). Built by Cantieri Navale Triestino for Cosulich Line. M.V Trieste - New York, 19 December 1928. Transferred to Italian Line 1932. Seized by American forces 1943; converted to troopship. Returned to Italian Line 1946. Resumed passenger service January 1947. Sold to Siosa Line 1965; renamed CARIBIA.

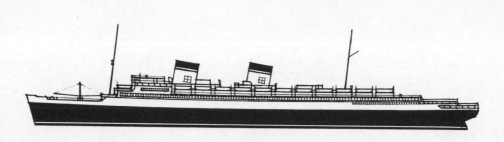

135 REX
'32, (1932-44) 51,062. 879 x 97. Quadruple screw, turbines, 28 knots. Laid down by S.A. Ansaldo, Sestri Ponente, for N.G.I.; transferred to Italian Line during construction. M.V. Genoa-New York, 27 September 1932. Broke the westbound speed record August 1933, making the crossing at an average speed of 28.92 knots. Bombed and sunk by British aircraft south of Trieste 9 September 1944; raised and broken up Yugoslavia 1947.

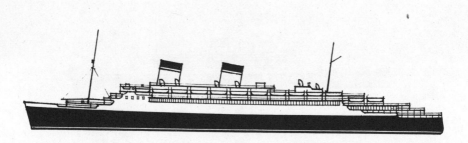

136 CONTE DI SAVOIA
'32, (1932-43) 48,502. 814 x 96. Quadruple screw, turbines, 27 knots. Laid down by Cantieri Riuniti dell' Adriatico, Monfalcone, for Lloyd Sabaudo; transferred to Italian Line during construction. The first Atlantic liner with gyro stabilizers. M.V. Genoa-New York, 30 November 1932. Bombed and sunk by American aircraft near Venice, 11 September 1943. Refloated October 1945; broken up Monfalcone 1950.

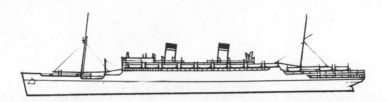

137 CONTE BIANCAMANO
'25, (1925-32) (1950-60) 23,842. 665 x 76. Twin screw turbines, 20 knots. Built by Wm
Beardmore & Co, Glasgow, for Lloyd Sabaudo. M.V. Genoa-New York, 20 November 1925.
Transferred to Italian Line 1932; placed on South American service. Sold to Lloyd Triestino
(Italy) 1937 for Far East service. Seized by United States forces at Colon, Panama Canal Zone
December 1941. Commissioned as U.S. Navy transport 1942; renamed U S S HERMITAGE
(AP-54). Returned to Italian Line 1947; renamed CONTE BIANCAMANO. Resumed South
American service, November 1949. Employed in North Atlantic summer service 1950-60.
Broken up La Spezia 1960.

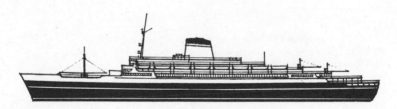

138 ANDREA DORIA
'53, (1953-56) 29,082. 700 x 90. Twin screw, turbines, 23 knots. Built by S.A. Ansaldo, Sestri
Ponente. M.V. Genoa-New York, 14 January 1953. Collided with Swedish American Liner
STOCKHOLM (240) in fog 50 miles off Nantucket Island on the night of 25 July 1956. Sank the
following day with a loss of 51 lives.

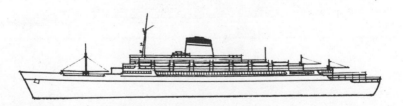

139 CRISTOFORO COLOMBO ●
'54, (1954-   ) 29,429. Details as (138). Built by S.A. Ansaldo, Sestri Ponente. M.V. Genoa-New
York, 15 July 1954.

73

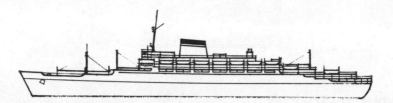

140 GIULIO CESARE ●
'51, (1956-60) 27,078. 680 x 87. Twin screw, motorship, 21 knots. Built by Cantieri Riuniti dell'
Adriatico, Monfalcone. M.V. Italy-South America, 27 October 1951. Transferred to North Atlantic
service 1956. F.V. Genoa-New York, 29 June 1956. Returned to River Plate service 1960.

141 AUGUSTUS (II) ●
'52, (1957-61) 27.090. Details as (140). Built by Cantieri Riuniti dell' Adriatico. M.V. Italy-South
America, March 1952. Transferred to North Atlantic service 1957. F.V. Genoa-New York, 7
February 1957. Returned to River Plate service 1961.

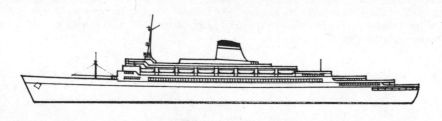

142 LEONARDO DA VINCI ●
'60, (1960-) 33,340. 767 x 92. Twin screw, turbines, 23 knots. Built by S.A. Ansaldo, Sestri
Ponente. M.V. Genoa-New York, 30 June 1960.

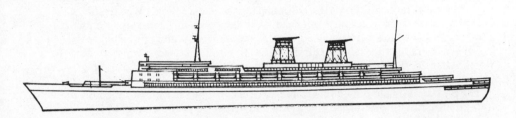

143 MICHELANGELO ●
'65, (1965-   ) 45,911. 905 x 102. Twin screw, turbines, 26 knots. Built by S.A. Ansaldo. M.V.
Genoa-New York, 12 May 1965.

144 RAFFAELLO ●
'65, (1965-   ) 45,933. Details as (143). Built by Cantieri dell' Adriatico, San Marco. M.V. Genoa-
New York, 25 July 1965.

FLOTTA LAURO, NAPLES (1953-56)

The Flotta Lauro was founded by Achille Lauro in 1923 to engage in tramping and trade between Italy and East Africa. Soon after the end of World War II, the Company bought three surplus American-built naval vessels, including two escort aircraft carriers which were renamed ROMA and SYDNEY and converted to passenger liners for the Italy - Australia trade. In 1953 they were transferred to the North Atlantic, running from Naples and Genoa to New York, with calls at Gibraltar, Barcelona and Halifax.

The SYDNEY made only a few round voyages, but her sister continued on the transatlantic run until returned to the Australian service at the end of 1956.

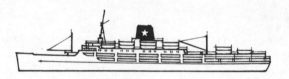

145 ROMA
'43, (1953-56) 14,976. 497 x 69. Single screw, turbines, 17 knots. Laid down as C-3 type cargo liner GLACIER by Seattle-Tacoma Shipbuilding Corp, Tacoma, Washington; completed as Royal Navy escort aircraft carrier H M S ATHELING. Returned to U S Navy 1946. Bought by Flotta Lauro 1950 and refitted for passenger service; renamed ROMA. Placed on Italy-Australia service, transferred to Atlantic. F.V. Naples-New York, May 1953. Returned to Australia service, December 1956. Broken up Savona 1967.

146 SYDNEY
'44, (1953) 14,986. Details as (145). Laid down as cargo liner CROATAN by Western Pipe and Steel Co., San Francisco, California. Completed as Royal Navy escort aircraft carrier H M S FENCER. Returned to U S Navy 1946. Bought by Flotta Lauro 1950 and refitted for passenger service; renamed SYDNEY. Placed on Italy-Australia service. Made a series of voyages, Liverpool to Quebec, in summer of 1953; returned to Australia service. Renamed ROMA after sister ship retired in 1967; engaged in cruising. Sold to Sovereign Cruises 1970; renamed GALAXY QUEEN.

SITMAR LINE, GENOA (1954-66)

The Societa Italiana Transporti Marittimi of Genoa, popularly known as the "Sitmar" Line, began a transatlantic passenger service with the transfer of the CASTEL FELICE from the South American service and her sailing from Bremen to Quebec on 13 July 1954. The CASTEL FELICE, built in 1930 as the British India Steam Navigation Co's KENYA for East African service, had after a somewhat checkered career, been purchased by Sitmar three years before.

She was joined in 1957 by the FAIRSEA, formerly the escort aircraft carrier U S S CHARGER, which made three round voyages. After 1958 both ships were transferred to the Europe - Australia trade and the North Atlantic service was limited to summer sailings by the CASTEL FELICE.

147 CASTEL FELICE
'30, (1954-66) 10,953. 493 x 64. Twin screw, turbines, 16 knots. Built by Alexander Stephen and Sons, Linthouse, Glasgow, as KENYA for British India Steam Navigation Co, (Great Britain). Converted to infantry landing ship 1940; renamed H M S KEREN. Bought by Alva Steamship Co, (Panama) 1949; renamed KENYA, then KEREN, then KENYA once more at short intervals. Renamed FAIRSTONE, 1950, reverting to KENYA a few months later. Again renamed KEREN 1951; transferred to Sitmar Line. Refitted at Genoa 1952; renamed CASTEL FELICE and placed on Italy-South America service. Transferred to North Atlantic; F.V. Bremen-Quebec, 13 July 1954. After 1958 operated primarily on Italy - Australia service with occasional transatlantic sailings. Registry transferred to Panama 1968. Broken up Kaohsiung. Taiwan 1970.

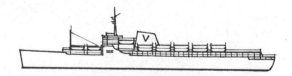

148 FAIRSEA
'41, (1957) 13,317. 492 x 70. Single screw, motorship, 16 knots. Launched by Sun Shipbuilding & Drydock Co, Chester, Pennsylvania as C-3 type cargo liner RIO DE LA PLATA for Moore - McCormack Line (United States). Completed as escort aircraft carrier U S S CHARGER (CVE-30) Bought by Sitmar Line and rebuilt as emigrant carrier 1949; renamed FAIRSEA. Refitted at Trieste and chartered by Australian Government for emigrant service 1955. Registry transferred to Panama 1968. Disabled by fire in engine room 900 miles west of Panama, 24 January 1969. Towed to Balboa by American freighter LOUISE LYKES; broken up La Spezia.

GRIMALDI-SIOSA LINE, PALERMO (1956-61)

The Fratelli Grimaldi of Genoa and their subsidiary, the Sicula Oceanica Societa per Azioni of Palermo, purchased three susplus passenger vessels in 1955-56 and refitted them for a service to Central America. Two of these, the former Transports Maritimes ships CAMPANA and FLORIDA built in the 1920s, were renamed IRPINIA and ASCANIA respectively.

The IRPINIA was transferred to the North Atlantic and sailed from Southampton for New York in October 1956. The following summer, the ASCANIA made a number of round voyages and between 1959 and 1961 both ships made periodic sailings from European ports to Montreal and Quebec. The transatlantic service ended when both ships were returned to the Central American trade, for which the IRPINIA was re-engined and radically reconstructed.

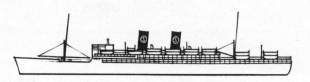

149 IRPINIA
'29, (1956-61) 12,279. 537 x 67. Twin screw, turbines, 19 knots. Built by Swan, Hunter & Wigham Richardson, as CAMPANA for Soc. Generale de Transports Maritimes (France). Sailed on South American service. Interned at Buenos Aires during World War II and requisitioned by Argentine Government 1943; renamed RIO JACHAL. Returned to owners 1946; renamed CAMPANA. Transferred to Far East service 1951. Bought by Grimaldi-Siosa Lines 1955; renamed IRPINIA. F.V. Southampton-New York, 6 October 1956. Extensively refitted, re-engined with diesels, and two funnels replaced with single streamlined stack at Trieste 1962; transferred to Caribbean service.

150 ASCANIA
'26, (1957-59) 9,536. 490 x 60. Twin screw, turbines, 14 knots. Built by Ateliers et Chantiers de la Loire, St Nazaire, as FLORIDA for Transports Maritimes. M.V. Marseilles-South America, 16 November 1926. Badly damaged in collision with British aircraft carrier H M S GLORIOUS off Gibralter, 1 April 1931. Sunk by German planes at Bone, 13 November 1942. Raised May 1944; reconditioned at Toulon; second funnel removed. Bought by Grimaldi-Siosa Lines 1955; renamed ASCANIA; Placed on Caribbean service. Transferred to run between Le Havre, Southampton and Quebec in summers of 1957 and 1959. Laid up at Spezia October 1967; broken up 1968

4 GERMANY

HAMBURG AMERICAN LINE, HAMBURG (1856-1914) (1921-39)

The Hamburg-Amerikanische Paketfahrt Aktien-Gesellschaft was founded in 1847
to operate a fleet of ships between Hamburg and New York, but it was not until
1 July 1856 that the first steamer, the BORUSSIA, sailed from Hamburg, followed
by the HAMMONIA a month later.

   With its rival, the Norddeutscher Lloyd, the Company served an increasing flood.
of emigrants from Northern Europe, and its fleet expanded enormously under the
guiding genius of Albert Ballin, one of the great names in shipping history. The Line's
prestige was further enhanced when the DEUTSCHLAND captured the "Blue
Riband", breaking both the westbound and eastbound speed records on her maiden
voyage in July 1900.

   By 1914 the Hamburg American Line was the largest ship-owning company in the
world, operating to all parts of the globe with over 1,400,000 tons of shipping,
including the IMPERATOR and VATERLAND, two new express liners of over
50,000 tons and of unprecedented luxury. A third, the BISMARCK, was nearing
completion. The First World War wiped out this huge fleet almost completely. Seven
vessels, including the VATERLAND and AMERIKA, were interned in American
ports and when the United States entered the war they were seized and converted to
transports. After the Armistice all the ships laid up in Germany were requisitioned
by the victorious Allies. The IMPERATOR was renamed BERENGARIA by the
Cunard Line while the BISMARCK became the White Star liner MAJESTIC.

   Despite these circumstances, an alliance with the United American Lines resulted
in a regular post-war service within two years, the first sailing under the German flag
being made by the BAYERN in September 1921. By 1926 the Company was able to
take over the United American Lines' RESOLUTE, RELIANCE and CLEVELAND,
augmenting them by the construction of eight new ships.

   World War II once more saw the complete destruction of the fleet, most of the
ships being lost through Allied air attack. In post-war years the Line built up a large
fleet of cargo vessels but the transatlantic service was never revived.

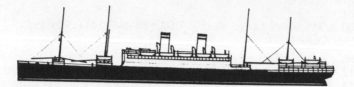

151 CLEVELAND

'09, (1909-19) (1926-33) 16,971. 588(R) x 65, Twin screw, quadruple expansion engines, 16 knots. Built by Blohm & Voss, Hamburg. M.V. Hamburg-New York, 27 March 1909. Lay idle in Hamburg throughout World War I. Surrendered to Allies, March 1919 and allocated to United States; converted to transport and renamed MOBILE. Transferred to British Government later in year.. Sold to Byron Line (Great Britain) 1920; renamed KING ALEXANDER. Sold to United American Lines (Panama) 1923; renamed CLEVELAND. Reverted to Hamburg American Line 1926. Laid up at Hamburg 1931; broken up 1933.

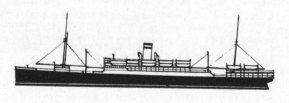

152 THURINGIA

'23, (1923-30) 11,343. 473(R) x 61. Single screw, turbines, 13 knots. Built by Howaldtswerke, Kiel. M.V. Hamburg-New York, 10 January 1923. Transferred to South American service 1930; renamed GENERAL SAN MARTIN. Sold to Hamburg-South American Line 1936. Seized by British Government 1945; renamed EMPIRE DEBEN. Broken up 1949.

153 WESTPHALIA

'23, (1923-30) 11,343. Details as (152) Built by Howaldtswerke. M.V. Hamburg-New York, 17 May 1923. Transferred to South American service 1930; renamed GENERAL ARTIGAS. Sold to Hamburg-South American Line 1936. Bombed and sunk by British aircraft at Hamburg 1943.

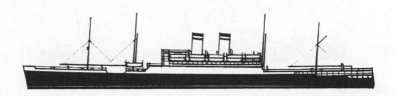

154 HANSA
'23, (1923-45) 21,131. 678 x 73. Twin screw, turbines, 20 knots. Built by Blohm & Voss as
ALBERT BALLIN. M.V. Hamburg-New York, 5 July 1923. Extensively rebuilt 1934; lengthened
by 43 feet. Renamed HANSA 1935. Sunk by mine off Warnemunde, 6 March 1945. Refloated by
Russians 1949; towed to Antwerp for rebuilding. Renamed SOVETSKY SOJUS 1950. Refit
completed at Warner Werft, Warnemunde. Badly damaged by fire 1954; returned to service
September 1955.

155 DEUTSCHLAND
'24, (1924-45) 21,046. Details as (154). Built by Blohm & Voss. M.V. Hamburg-New York, 27
March 1924. Lengthened by 43 feet 1934. Sunk by Allied air attack off Neustadt, 3 May 1945.

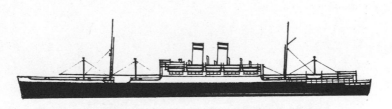

156 HAMBURG
'26, (1926-45) 22,117. 681 x 72. Twin screw, turbines, 20 knots. Built by Blohm & Voss. M.V.
Hamburg-New York, 9 April 1926. Lengthened by 43 feet 1933. Sunk by floating mine near
Sassnitz, 7 March 1945. Refloated by Russians 1950 and converted to whale-oil factory ship;
renamed YURI DOLGORUKI.

157 NEW YORK
'27, (1927-45) 22,337. Details as (156). Built by Blohm & Voss. M.V. Hamburg-New York, 13 May
1927. Lengthened by 43 feet 1934. Left New York for Hamburg by way of Murmansk, 28 August
1939; arrived 13 December after evading British fleet. Bombed and sunk at Kiel, 3 April 1945.
Refloated, towed to England and broken up 1948.

158 RESOLUTE

'20, (1926-35) 19,653. 616 x 72. Triple screw, combination triple expansion engines and turbine, 17 knots. Laid down 1914 by A.G. Weser, Bremen, as WILLIAM O'SWALD, work halted by war. Incomplete hull allotted to Royal Holland Lloyd (Netherlands) as reparation 1916; renamed BRABANTIA. Construction completed 1920; placed on Rotterdam-South American service. Sold to United American Lines (United States) 1922; renamed RESOLUTE. F.V. Hamburg-New York, 11 April 1922. Transferred to Panamanian registry 1923 to avoid restrictions of Prohibition — the first Atlantic liner to run under a flag of convenience. Reverted to Hamburg American Line 1926; used extensively for cruising. Sold to Italian Government 1935; renamed LOMBARDIA. Served as transport and in carrying settlers to Libya. Set afire and sunk by Allied air attack at Naples, 4 August 1943; hulk raised and broken up 1947.

159 RELIANCE

'20, (1926-38) 19,582. Details as (158). Laid down 1914 by J.C. Tecklenborg A.G., Geestemunde, as JOHANN HEINRICH BURCHARD; construction halted by war. Incomplete hull allotted to Royal Holland Lloyd; renamed LIMBURGIA. Sold to United American Lines 1922; renamed RELIANCE. F.V. Hamburg-New York, 3 May 1922. Transferred to Panamanian registry 1923. Reverted to Hamburg American Line 1926. Gutted by fire at Hamburg, 8 August 1938, and became a total loss; broken up 1941.

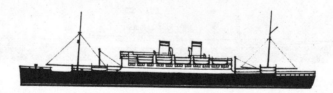

160 MILWAUKEE

'29, (1929-45) 16,699. 574 x 72. Twin screw, motorship, 16 knots. Built by Blohm & Voss, Hamburg. M.V. Hamburg-New York, 11 June 1929. Allocated to British Government 1945; renamed EMPIRE WAVENEY. Destroyed by fire at Liverpool while fitting out as troopship, 1 March 1946; hulk broken up 1947.

161 ST. LOUIS

'29, (1929-44) 16,732. Details as (160). Built by Bremer Vulkan, Vegesack. M.V. Hamburg-New York 23 March 1929. Served as German Navy accommodation ship at Kiel; severely damaged by Allied air attacks, 30 August 1944. Hulk towed to Hamburg 1946 and converted to hotel ship; broken up 1950.

NORDDEUTSCHER LLOYD, BREMEN (1858-1914) (1922-39) (1954-)

The North German Lloyd was formed in 1856 to provide a shipping service between Bremen and New York. Orders were placed for four iron screw steamers and the first sailing was made by the BREMEN, which left Bremerhaven 19 June 1858. Within a few years, a regular bi-weekly service was in operation and new shipping routes were being established throughout the world.

Toward the end of the nineteenth century a large programme of ship replacement was undertaken which included the outstanding ship of the decade, the KAISER WILHELM DER GROSSE, which made the westbound crossing on her maiden voyage in 1897 at an average speed of 21.39 knots to make her the fastest as well as the largest ship afloat. Record crossings were also made by the KRONPRINZ WILHELM in 1902 and the KAISER WILHELM II two years later.

In 1913 the Line carried 240,000 transatlantic passengers, while the fleet consisted of nearly 800,000 gross tons of shipping with 100,000 tons under construction, second only to that of the rival Hamburg American Line.

In World War I, nine ships were interned in American ports and were eventually seized as transports under the American flag. Of those in home ports, the KAISER WILHELM DER GROSSE was fitted out as an armed merchant cruiser and was sunk by H M S HIGHFLYER at Rio de Oro, West Africa. All the Line's remaining ships were seized by the Allies after the Armistice.

Service was re-established with the repurchase of units of the Line's pre-war fleet, the SEYDLITZ sailing from Bremerhaven in February 1922. A year later the MUNCHEN was commissioned as well as the COLUMBUS, laid down before the war but allowed to remain in Germany. As a result of this successful recovery, the Line ordered two 50,000 ton express liners. The first of these, the BREMEN, on her maiden voyage broke the speed record which had been held for twenty years by the MAURETANIA, while her sister, the EUROPA, captured the "Blue Riband" the following year.

The Line lost its entire fleet for a second time in World War II, either through sinking or confiscation. It was not until 1954 that the Swedish American Line's GRIPSHOLM was purchased and renamed BERLIN to revive the transatlantic passanger service. The BERLIN was retired in 1955 and replaced by the EUROPA, the former Swedish American liner KUNGSHOLM, which currently serves as a running mate for the BREMEN, formerly the Cie. Sud-Atlantique's PASTEUR, purchased in 1957 and placed in service two years later.

162 SEYDLITZ
'03, (1922-29) 7,942. 470 x 55. Twin screw, triple expansion engines, 14 knots. Built by
F. Schichau, Danzig, for Far East service. Left Sydney at outbreak of World War I to accompany
Admiral von Spee's squadron around the Horn. Escaped destruction at Battle of Falklands and
took refuge in Bahia Blanca for duration of war. Reverted to Norddeutscher Lloyd 1921; F.V.
Bremen-New York, 21 February 1922. Transferred to Cuban service 1929. Broken up
Bremerhaven 1931.

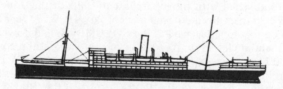

163 YORCK
'06, (1922-29) 8,976. 481 x 57. Twin screw quadruple expansion engines, 14 knots. Built by
F. Schichau for Far East service. Left Tsingtau, August 1914 to act as supply ship for Admiral
von Spee's squadron. When empty sailed to Valparaiso for interment. F.V. Bremen - New York,
11 March 1922. Transferred to Cuban service 1929. Broken up Danzig 1932.

164 DERFFLINGER
'07, (1923-32) 9,144. Details as (163). Built by F Schichau. With LUTZOW sought refuge in
Suez Canal at outbreak of World War I 1914. Forced to sea and captured by British forces;
renamed HUNTSGREEN. Reverted to Norddeutscher Lloyd 1923; renamed DERFFLINGER.
F.V. Bremen-New York, 1923. Broken up Bremerhaven 1932.

165 LUTZOW
'08, (1924-32) 8,818. Details as (163). Built by A.G. Weser, Bremen. Captured by British, October
1914; renamed HUNTSEND. Reverted to Norddeutscher Lloyd 1924; renamed LUTZOW. F.V.
Bremen-New York, 1924. Broken up Bremen 1933

84

166 KARLSRUHE (II)

'00. (1923-32) 10,881. 545 x 60. Twin screw, quadruple expansion engines, 15 knots. Built by A.G. Vulkan, Stettin, as PRINZESS IRENE for Far East service. Interned at New York at outbreak of World War I. Confiscated by United States Government to serve as troopship 1917; renamed POCAHONTAS. Repurchased by Norddeutscher Lloyd 1923; renamed BREMEN (III). F.V. Bremen-New York, April 1923. Renamed KARLSRUHE 1928 to allow use of name for new express liner. Broken up Bremerhaven 1932.

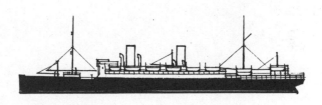

167 MUNCHEN (II)

'23, (1923-31) 13,325. 551 x 65. Twin screw, triple expansion engines, 16 knots. Built by A.G. Vulkan; the first post-war construction by Norddeutscher Lloyd. M.V. Bremen-New York, 14 September 1923. Gutted by fire at New York 1930. Rebuilt at Bremen 1931; renamed GENERAL VON STEUBEN (174).

168 STUTTGART (II)

'24, (1924-32) 13,367. Details as (167) Built by A.G. Vulkan. M.V. Bremen-New York, 15 January 1924. Transferred to Far East Service 1932. Bombed and sunk by Allied air attack at Gdynia, 9 October 1943.

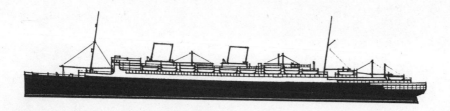

169 COLUMBUS (II)
'23, (1923-39) 32,354. 775 x 83. Twin screw, turbines, 23 knots. Laid down 1914 as HINDENBURG by F. Schichau, Danzig. Construction halted by war. Still on ways at time of Armistice; company allowed to retain possession. Completed as COLUMBUS, taking former name of HOMERIC, sister ship ceded to Great Britain as war reparation. M.V. Bremen-New York, November 1923. Extensively altered 1929; reciprocating engines replaced by turbines, refitted for oil fuel, funnels shortened. At outbreak of World War II took temporary refuge in Vera Cruz, but was intercepted off the Virginia coast by HMS Hyperion 19 December 1939; scuttled by crew to avoid capture.

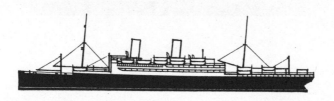

170 BERLIN (II)
'25, (1925-45) 15,286. 571 x 69. Twin screw, triple expansion engines, 16 knots. Built by Bremer Vulkan, Vegesack. M.V. Bremen-New York, 1925. Rescued survivors of sinking liner VESTRIS off Virginia Capes, 12 November 1928. Served as hospital ship in Norwegian waters during war. Sunk by mine off Swinemunde, 1 February 1945. Hulk raised by Russians 1949; renamed ADMIRAL NAKHIMOV. Reconstruction completed at Warnemunde 1957.

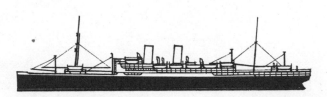

171 DRESDEN (II)

'15, (1927-34) 14,588. 570 x 67. Twin screw, quadruple expansion engines, 15 knots. Built by
Bremer Vulkan as ZEPPELIN for Australia trade. Turned over to Allies as reparation 1919. Bought
by Orient Line (Great Britain) 1921; renamed ORMUZ. Repurchased by Norddeutscher Lloyd
1927; renamed DRESDEN. F.V. Bremen-New York, 1927. Employed extensively in cruising after
1930. Struck submerged rock while on cruise in Bokn Fjord, Norway, 20 June 1934. Beached and
landed passengers but sank the following day.

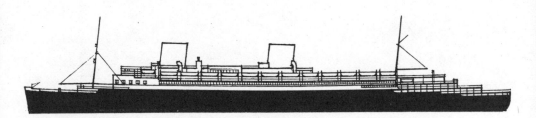

172 BREMEN (IV)

'29, (1929-42) 51,656. 938 x 101. Quadruple screw, turbines, 26 knots. Built by A.G. Weser,
Bremen. M.V. Bremen-New York, 16 July 1929 in record breaking time, making the crossing
at an average speed of 27.83 knots to win the "Blue Riband". At the outbreak of World War II,
sailed to Germany from New York by way of Murmansk and along the Norwegian coast,
successfully eluding interception. Gutted by fire believed to have been set by member of the crew
at Bremerhaven, 18 March 1942. Found to be beyond repair and stripped to water line; broken up
1953.

173 EUROPA (I)

'30, (1930-46) 49,746. 936 x 102. Details as (172). Built by Blohm & Voss, Hamburg. Launched
the day before BREMEN but construction delayed for nearly a year by serious fire in yard. M.V.
Bremen-New York, 19 March 1930, breaking BREMEN's westbound record at an average speed of
27.91 knots. Remained in German ports throughout the war. Turned over to French Government
as reparation 1946. Assigned to French Line; renamed LIBERTE (198).

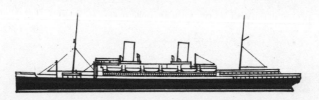

174 GENERAL VON STEUBEN
'23, (1931-38) 14,690. Formerly MUNCHEN (167); renamed GENERAL VON STEUBEN 1931.
Designated as Nazi "Strength Through Joy" cruise ship 1938; renamed STEUBEN. Sunk by
Russian submarine in the Baltic Sea with loss of over 3,000 lives while transporting refugees from
East Prussia, 10 February 1945.

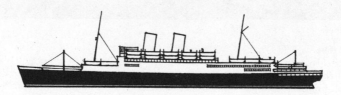

175 BERLIN (III)
'25, (1955-66) 18,600. Formerly GRIPSHOLM (238) Swedish American Line. Bought by
Norddeutscher Lloyd 1954; renamed BERLIN 1955. F.V. Bremen-New York, 8 January 1955.
Broken up La Spezia 1966.

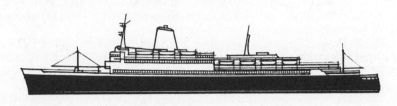

176 BREMEN (V) ●
'39, (1959-   ) 32,360. 697 x 90. Quadruple screw, turbines, 23 knots. Built by Chantiers de
Penhoet, St Nazaire, as PASTEUR for Cie. Sud-Atlantique (France). Scheduled M.V. Bordeaux-
Buenos Aires, cancelled by outbreak of war 1939. Carried 400 tons of Banque de France gold
reserve to Canada, June 1940. Seized two months later by British and operated as troopship 1940-
45; subsequently continued as transport under French flag during war in Indo-China. Bought by
Norddeutscher Lloyd 1957; refitted at Bremerhaven over a period of nearly two years. Renamed
BREMEN 1959. F.V. Bremen-New York, 9 July 1959.

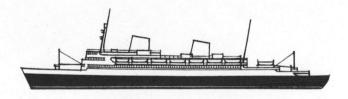

177 EUROPA (II) ●
'53, (1966-   ) 21,514. Formerly KUNGSHOLM (241) Swedish American Line. Bought by
Norddeutscher Lloyd 1965; renamed EUROPA. F.V. Bremen-New York, 9 January 1966.

BERNSTEIN LINE, HAMBURG (1931-39)

The Arnold Bernstein Reederei was founded in 1926 as a cargo service between Antwerp and New York, using second-hand tonnage. Under an agreement with the Erie Railroad in the United States, the Company specialized in shipping uncrated American automobiles to Europe.

In 1928-29 three ships were bought from the Shaw Savill Line and in 1931 they were refitted to provide passenger accommodation. Four years later the Red Star liners PENNLAND and WESTERNLAND were purchased and their sailings from Antwerp were continued under the name Bernstein (Red Star) Line.

Herr Bernstein was imprisoned by the Nazis as a non-Aryan in 1937 and within two years the Line was disbanded. The PENNLAND and WESTERNLAND were sold to the Holland-America Line, while the remaining ships were sold for cargo service or for breaking up.

178 GEROLSTEIN
'04 (1931-39) 6,845. 454(R) x 56. Twin screw, quadruple expansion engines, 13 knots. Built by
Harland & Wolff, Belfast, as MAMARI for Shaw Savill Line (Great Britain). Purchased by Arnold
Bernstein 1928; renamed GEROLSTEIN and operated as cargo ship. Passenger accommodation
installed 1931. Bernstein fleet disbanded 1939. Sold to H.C. Horn Co (Germany) 1939; renamed
CONSUL HORN. Mined off Borkum Island, July 1942.

179 ILSENSTEIN
'04, (1931-39) 6,518. 448(R) x 56. Twin screw, triple expansion engines, 13 knots. Built by
Workman, Clark & Co, Belfast, as MATATUA for Shaw Savill Line. Purchased by Arnold Bernstein
1928; renamed ILSENSTEIN and operated as a cargo ship. Passenger accommodation installed
1931. Withdrawn from service 1939 and sold for breaking up. Arrived at Blyth but demolition
halted and towed to Scapa Flow February 1940 for use as block-ship; demolished 1950.

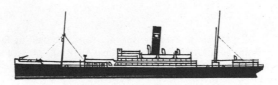

180 KONIGSTEIN
'07, (1931-39) 7,415. 480 x 60. Twin screw, triple expansion engines, 14 knots. Built by Swan,
Hunter & Wigham Richardson, Wallsend-on-Tyne, as ARAWA for Shaw Savill Line. Engaged in
passenger service to New Zealand. Purchased by Arnold Bernstein 1928; renamed KONIGSTEIN
and operated as cargo ship. Passenger accommodation reinstalled 1931. Sold to shipbreakers at
Ghent 1939. Owing to wartime shipping shortage, demolition stopped and reconverted to cargo
ship; renamed GANDIA. Chartered to Cie. Maritime Belge (Belgium) December 1939. Torpedoed
and sunk in North Atlantic with loss of 65 lives, 22 January 1942.

EUROPE-CANADA LINE, BREMEN (1955-66)

The Company, a subsidiary of the Holland-America Line, inaugurated a service
between Bremen and Quebec and Montreal in 1955 with the motorship SEVEN
SEAS, formerly the NELLY of the Caribbean Land & Shipping Corp. registered in
Panama. The first sailing from Bremen was on 30 April 1955.

Transatlantic services were irregular and included charters as well as cruising. They
concluded with the sale of the SEVEN SEAS in 1966.

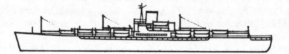

181   SEVEN SEAS
'40, (1955-66) 12,575. 492 x 69. Single screw, motorship, 16 knots. Built by Sun Shipbuilding &
Dry Dock Co, Chester, Pennsylvania, as C-3 type cargo liner MORMACMAIL for Moore-
McCormack Lines (United States). Converted to U.S. Navy escort aircraft carrier 1941; renamed
U S S LONG ISLAND (CVE-1). Bought by Caribbean Land & Shipping Corp. (Panama) and
refitted as emigrant ship 1949; renamed NELLY. Bought by Europe-Canada Line 1954; renamed
SEVEN SEAS. F.V. Bremen-Montreal, 30 April 1955. Registry transferred to West Germany 1955.
Converted to student hostel at University of Rotterdam, September 1966.

GERMAN ATLANTIC LINE,   HAMBURG   (1958-   )

The Hamburg Atlantic Line purchased the Canadian Pacific liner EMPRESS OF SCOTLAND in January 1958. She was renamed HANSEATIC and drastically altered in an extensive refit. Her first sailing, from Hamburg to New York, was on 21 July 1958.

In September 1966, the HANSEATIC caught fire at her dock in New York while preparing to sail and was towed to Hamburg a month later to be broken up. As a replacement the Company, now known as the Deutsche Atlantik Linie, purchased the recently-built Zim liner SHALOM which was renamed HANSEATIC to continue the name.

A new ship was ordered, the first liner to be built in West Germany since World War II. Completed in 1969, she was named the HAMBURG and immediately sailed on a series of long-range cruises.

The HANSEATIC and HAMBURG are numbered among the finest cruise liners afloat and their infrequent transatlantic crossings are incidental to their cruising schedules.

182 HANSEATIC (I)
'30, (1958-66) 30,029. Formerly EMPRESS OF SCOTLAND (87) Canadian Pacific. Bought by
Hamburg Atlantic Line 1958; temporarily renamed SCOTLAND. Completely reconstructed at
Hamburg; renamed HANSEATIC. F.V. Hamburg-New York, 21 July 1958. Severely damaged
by fire at dock in New York, 7 September 1966. Towed to Hamburg for repairs but broken up
after survey revealed extent of damage.

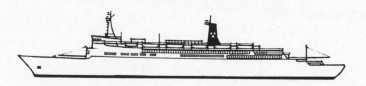

183 HANSEATIC (II) ●
'64, (1968-   ) 25,320. Formerly SHALOM (273) Zim Lines. Bought by German Atlantic Line
1967; renamed HANSEATIC. F.V. Hamburg-New York, 23 May 1968.

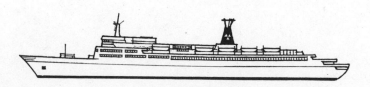

184 HAMBURG ●
'69, (1969-   ) 25,022. 638 x 87. Twin screw, turbines, 23 knots. Built by Howaldtswerke-
Deutsche Werft A.G., Hamburg. M.V. Hamburg-South America, 30 March 1969. F.V. Hamburg-
New York, 19 June 1969. Engaged almost exclusively in cruising.

5 FRANCE

COMPAGNIE GENERALE TRANSATLANTIQUE, PARIS (1864-)

The French Line, as the Company is commonly known, came into existence in 1861 under a mail contract with the government of Napoleon II. Its first North Atlantic sailing, from Le Havre to New York, was made by the paddle steamer WASHINGTON on 15 June 1864. During the next fifty years a large fleet of passenger and cargo steamers was built up for the transatlantic trade as well as for services to Mexico and the West Indies.

The Company lost a number of ships to enemy action during World War I, including the Atlantic liner LA PROVENCE. Steps were taken at the close of hostilities to replace the lost tonnage, including the acquisition of three ex-German vessels which were renamed SUFFREN, ROUSSILLON and LA BOURDONNAIS. In addition, the PARIS, which had been lying in an incomplete state throughout the war, was placed in service.

In the late twenties and early thirties the Line introduced a series of four ships notable for their comfort and luxury, beginning with the ILE DE FRANCE and culminating in the revolutionary NORMANDIE which broke all existing speed records on her maiden voyage.

In 1938, the LAFAYETTE was destroyed by fire while in dry dock at Le Havre, and within a year the PARIS was gutted by fire at her berth in the same port. However, these tragedies were overshadowed when the NORMANDIE caught fire while being converted to a troopship in New York in 1942 and, as a result of the tons of water with which she was flooded by firemen, capsized and sank. Despite enormous salvage efforts she never sailed again.

The CHAMPLAIN and DE GRASSE were sunk by enemy action during World War II. The latter however, was refloated and inaugurated the Company's post-war sailings in 1947. As war reparation, the Company acquired the Norddeutscher Lloyd liner EUROPA which joined the fleet as LIBERTE after an extensive two-year refit beset by troubles.

In 1962 the flagship FRANCE, the last word in seagoing luxury made her maiden voyage. She remains today the only ship of the Line on the North Atlantic service.

185 LA SAVOIE

'01, (1901-27) 11,168. 580 x 60. Twin screw, triple expansion engines, 21 knots. Built by Cie. Generale Transatlantique (Penhoet) St Nazaire. M.V. Le Havre-New York, 31 March 1901. Served as armed merchant cruiser 1914-18. Returned to passenger service April 1919. Withdrawn from service October 1927, after 446 crossings; broken up Dunkirk 1928.

186 CHICAGO

'08, (1908-28) 9,350. 524 x 57. Twin screw, triple expansion engines, 16 knots. Built by Ateliers et Chantiers de l' Atlantique, St Nazaire. M.V. Le Havre-New York, 30 May 1908. Reconstructed for West Indies service 1928; renamed GUADELOUPE. Broken up St Nazaire 1936.

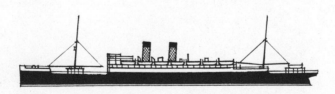

187 ROCHAMBEAU

'11, (1911-34) 12,678. 559(R) x 63. Quadruple screw, combination triple expansion engines and turbine, 15 knots. Built by Soc. des Chantiers et Ateliers de St Nazaire, Penhoet. M.V. Le Havre-New York, 16 September 1911. Broken up Dunkirk 1934.

188 FRANCE (II)

'12, (1912-34) 23,666. 720 x 76. Quadruple screw, turbines, 24 knots. Laid down by Chantiers et Ateliers de St Nazaire, as PICARDIE; renamed during construction. By far the largest and fastest French Line ship yet built. M.V. Le Havre-New York, 20 April 1912. Commissioned as FRANCE IV for service as troopship and hospital ship 1914. Resumed passenger service August 1919. Laid up at Le Havre September 1932; broken up Dunkirk 1934.

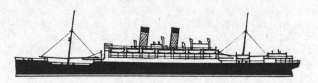

189 SUFFREN

'02, (1920-29) 12,350. 550 x 62. Twin screw, quadruple expansion engines, 15 knots. Built by Blohm & Voss, Hamburg, as BLUCHER for Hamburg American Line. Interned in Recife, Brazil, 1917 and confiscated by Brazilian Government; renamed LEOPOLDINA. Chartered by French Line for North Atlantic service 1920. Purchased 1923; renamed SUFFREN. F.V. Le Havre-New York, 8 May 1923. Broken up Genoa 1929.

190 ROUSSILLON

'06, (1920-31) 8,800. 482 x 58. Twin screw, quadruple expansion engines, 14 knots. Built by A.G. Weser, Bremen, as GOEBEN for Norddeutscher Lloyd. Acquired by French Line 1920; renamed ROUSSILLON. F.V. Le Havre-New York, 1920. Broken up Pasajes, Spain, 1931.

191 LA BOURDONNAIS

'04, (1921-33) 8,287. 472 x 56. Twin screw, triple expansion engines, 14 knots. Built by J.C. Tecklenborg, Geestemunde, as SCHARNHORST for Norddeutscher Lloyd. Acquired by French Line 1921; renamed LA BOURDONNAIS. F.V. Le Havre-New York, 2 April 1921. Withdrawn from service 1933; broken up Genoa 1934.

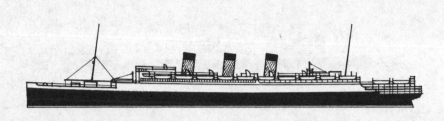

192 PARIS

'21, (1921-39) 34,569. 765 x 85. Quadruple screw, turbines, 22 knots. Laid down 1913 by Soc. des Chantiers et Ateliers de St Nazaire, Penhoet; construction delayed by war. Launched September 1916; hull then towed to Quiberon Bay for duration of war. Work resumed 1918. M.V. Le Havre-New York, 15 June 1921. Refitted after serious fire at Le Havre 1929. Gutted by fire, 20 April 1939; capsized and sank at berth in Le Havre where she lay throughout World War II. Hulk cleared 1947.

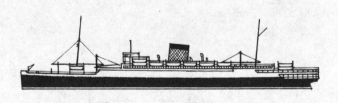

193 DE GRASSE

'24, (1924-40) (1947-52) 18,435. 574 x 71. Twin screw, turbines, 16 knots. Laid down 1920 as SUFFREN by Cammell Laird & Co, Birkenhead; renamed during construction, which required nearly four years. M.V. Le Havre-New York, 21 August 1924. Seized by Germans 1940; converted to accommodation ship at Bordeaux. Sunk by gunfire, 30 August 1944. Raised and refitted at St Nazaire 1945; one funnel removed. Resumed passenger service 12 July 1947. Transferred to West Indies service 1952. Sold to Canadian Pacific 1953; renamed EMPRESS OF AUSTRALIA (88).

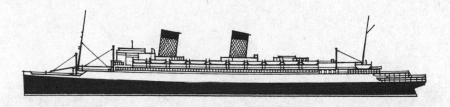

194 ILE DE FRANCE

'27, (1927-58) 44,356. 792 x 92. Quadruple screw, turbines, 24 knots. Built by Soc. des Chantiers
et Ateliers de St Nazaire, Penhoet. M.V. Le Havre-New York, 22 June 1927. One of the most
famous and popluar liners of the pre-war period. Converted to troopship by French Government
1940. After fall of France seized by British forces at Singapore and served as Free French transport
throughout war. Resumed temporary passenger service 1946; later returned to trooping to Indo-
China until April 1947. Completely reconditioned at St Nazaire 1947-49; funnels reduced to two.
F.V. Le Havre-New York, 21 July 1949. Withdrawn from service November 1958. Sailed as
FURANZU MARU February 1959 on delivery voyage to Osaka for breaking up.

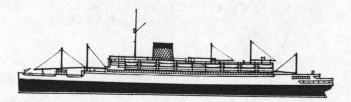

195 LAFAYETTE

'30, (1930-38) 25,178. 613 x 77. Quadruple screw, motorship, 18 knots. Built by Chantiers et
Ateliers de St Nazaire. M.V. Le Havre-New York, 17 May 1930. Destroyed by fire while in drydock
at Le Havre, 5 May 1938; hulk broken up Rotterdam.

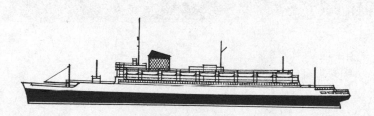

196 CHAMPLAIN

'32, (1932-40) 28,124. 641 x 83. Twin screw, turbines, 19 knots. Built by Soc. des Chantiers et
Ateliers de St Nazaire, Penhoet. M.V. Le Havre-New York, 18 June 1932. Sunk by magnetic mine
off La Pallice, 17 June 1940.

197 NORMANDIE

'35, (1935-41) 82,799. 1,027 x 118. Quadruple screw, turbo-electric, 30 knots. Built by Chantiers et Ateliers de St Nazaire. M.V. Le Havre-New York, 29 May 1935, breaking the westbound transatlantic record at an average speed of 29.98 knots and the eastbound record on the return crossing at 30.31 knots. Superstructure enlarged 1936, making her the largest ship in the world as well as one of the most luxurious ever built. Taken over by the United States Government for service as troopship 1941; renamed LAFAYETTE. Caught fire, 9 February 1942 during conversion at pier in New York; capsized and sank. Eventually refloated, towed to Port Newark, New Jersey for breaking up 1946.

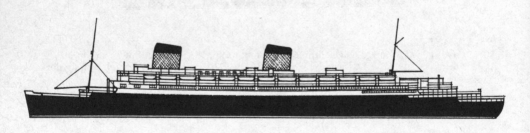

198 LIBERTE

'28, (1950-61) 51,839. Formerly EUROPA (173) Norddeutscher Lloyd. Awarded to France as reparation 1946; renamed LIBERTE. Broke loose from moorings in gale while being refitted at Le Havre, 9 December 1946; scuttled to prevent capsizing. Refloated and reconstruction begun at St Nazaire 1947; passenger service not resumed until 17 August 1950. Restaurant in First Class reputed to be the finest afloat. Broken up La Spezia 1962.

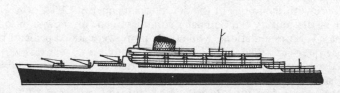

199 FLANDRE
'52, (1952-63) 20,459. 600 x 80. Twin screw, turbines, 22 knots. Built by Ateliers et Chantiers de France, Dunkirk. M.V. Le Havre-New York, 23 July 1952. Returned to builders for extensive repairs; resumed service 1953. Transferred to West Indies service 1963. Sold to Costa Line (Italy) 1968; renamed CARLA C. Chartered by Princess Cruises for cruising service out of Los Angeles; reverted to Costa Line 1970.

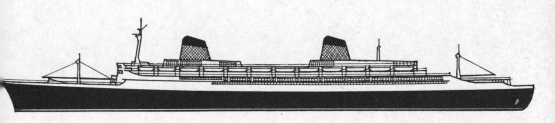

200 FRANCE (III) ●
'62, (1962-   ) 66,348. 1,035 x 110. Quadruple screw, turbines, 31 knots. Built by Chantiers de l' Atlantique (Penhoet-Loire), St Nazaire. F.V. Le Havre-New York, 3 February 1962. The longest passenger ship in the world.

FABRE LINE, MARSEILLES (1882-1931)

Cyprien Fabre et Cie. of Marseilles, which had been operating small steamers in the Mediterranean since 1874, began after a couple of experimental voyages, a Marseilles-New York service with the sailing of the 2,500 ton steamer SCOTIA in April 1882.

At the turn of the century the Company commissioned four new ships of larger size and increased accommodations, while three more were added prior to World War I, including the three-funnelled PATRIA. The Company's only war loss was the SANT' ANNA, torpedoed in the Mediterranean, but the VENEZIA was destroyed by fire in the North Atlantic the following year.

The PATRIA's sister ship, the PROVIDENCE, joined the fleet in 1920 and in the next few years the Company's services were extended to the Eastern Mediterranean with calls to embark emigrants at Piraeus, Istanbul and Levantine ports.

As a result of the economic slump in the 1930s, the PATRIA and PROVIDENCE were chartered to the Messageries Maritimes and the recently purchased ALESIA was laid up at Marseilles. Transatlantic passenger services were discontinued at the end of 1931 and, although the Line continued in operation, were never resumed.

201 CANADA
'12, (1912-31) 9,684. 490 x 56. Twin screw, triple expansion engines, 16 knots. Built by Forges et Chantiers de la Mediterranee, La Seyne. M.V. Marseilles-New York, 3 March 1912. Transferred to West Africa service 1931. Broken up Newport 1952.

202 PATRIA
'14, (1914-31) 11,885. 512 x 59. Twin screw, triple expansion engines, 16 knots. Built by Forges et Chantiers de la Mediterranee. M.V. Marseilles-New York, 11 April 1914. Chartered to Messageries Maritimes (France) 1932; sold to the same company 1940. Sunk by explosion in harbour of Haifa, Palestine, with heavy loss of life, 26 November 1940.

203 PROVIDENCE
'20, (1920-31) 11,996. Details as (202). Launched August 1914 by Forges et Chantiers de la Mediterranee; construction halted by war. M.V. Marseilles-New York, 1 June 1920. Chartered to Messageries Maritimes 1932; sold to same company 1940. Broken up La Spezia 1951.

204 SINAIA

'24, (1924-31) 8,567. 459 x 56. Twin screw, triple expansion engines, 14 knots. Built by Barclay, Curle & Co, Glasgow. M.V. Marseilles-New York, 25 September 1924. Scuttled by Germans at Marseilles, August 1944; raised and broken up 1947.

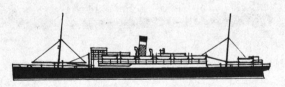

205 ALESIA

'06, (1928-33) 9,749. Formerly MONTREAL (73) Canadian Pacific. Bought by Fabre Line 1928; renamed ALESIA. F.V. Marseilles-New York, 6 July 1928. Laid up at Marseilles, April 1931; broken up Genoa 1933.

6 NETHERLANDS

HOLLAND-AMERICA LINE, ROTTERDAM (1872-)

The Nederlandsch-Amerikaansche Stoomvaart-Maatschappij, popularly known as the Holland-America Line, was founded in 1873, although a sailing had already been made from Rotterdam to New York by the 1,700 ton steamer ROTTERDAM on 15 October 1872, followed by a sister ship the MAAS.

In the Company's early years, the silting up of the New Waterway which connects the port of Rotterdam with the North Sea, severely limited the size of vessels using it. Alternate sailings were made from Amsterdam until 1892 when dredging operations permitted the passage of ships of deeper draft.

Neutral registry in World War I brought large profits and put the Company in a position to expand. However, construction of the STATENDAM was delayed as a result of American immigration restrictions. Despite the economic depression of the 1930s, a new flagship, the NIEUW AMSTERDAM, was commissioned in 1938.

When the Germans invaded Holland in May of 1940, they seized the VOLENDAM, while the STATENDAM was destroyed in the fighting. The Line's remaining vessels were chartered for service in the Allied war effort. The NIEUW AMSTERDAM in particular, had a spectacular war career, performing trooping duties throughout the world until her triumphant return to her home port in April 1946. The WESTERDAM and her sister ZUIDERDAM under construction at the time of the occupation, were repeatedly sabotaged by the Dutch underground to prevent their use by the Germans.

The post-war construction programme added a series of modern liners, and today the Company's fleet is engaged primarily in long-range cruising.

206 RIJNDAM
'01, (1901-29) 12,535. 570 x 62. Twin screw, triple expansion engines, 15 knots. Built by Harland & Wolff, Belfast. M.V. Rotterdam-New York, 10 October 1901. Requisitioned by United States Government for conversion to troopship 1918. Broken up Rotterdam 1929.

207 NOORDAM (I)
'02, (1902-27) 12,528. Details as (206). Built by Harland & Wolff. M.V. Rotterdam-New York, 1 May 1902. Laid up after mine damage 1917. Resumed passenger service March 1919. Chartered by Swedish American Line 1923; renamed KUNGSHOLM. Reverted to Holland-America Line 1925; renamed NOORDAM. Broken up Rotterdam 1928.

208 NIEUW AMSTERDAM (I)
'06, (1906-32) 17,149. 615 x 69. Twin screw, quadruple expansion engines, 16 knots. Built by Harland & Wolff. M.V. Rotterdam-New York, 7 April 1906. The only liner to maintain regular passenger sailings throughout World War I. Broken up Osaka 1932.

209 ROTTERDAM (IV)
'08, (1908-39) 24,149. 668 x 77. Twin screw, quadruple expansion engines, 18 knots. Built by Harland & Wolff, Belfast. M.V. Rotterdam-New York, 13 June 1908. The first North Atlantic liner with a glazed promenade deck. Laid up at Rotterdam 1916; returned to passenger service February 1919. Broken up Rotterdam 1940.

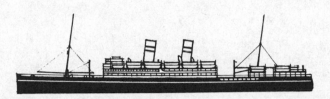

210 VOLENDAM

'22, (1922-51) 15,434. 576 x 67. Twin screw, turbines, 15 knots. Built by Harland & Wolff. M.V. Rotterdam-New York, 4 November 1922. Taken over by British Government 1940; converted to troopship. Torpedoed 300 miles off Irish coast while evacuating children to Canada, 30 August 1940; only one life lost as a result of disciplined removal of passengers and crew. Taken in tow and beached on the Isle of Bute; under repair for ten months. Partially reconditioned and resumed passenger service 1947. Laid up at Rotterdam November 1951; broken up three months later.

211 VEENDAM (II)

'23, (1923-53) 15,450. Details as (210). Built by Harland & Wolff. M.V. Rotterdam-New York, 18 April 1923. Seized by Germans at Rotterdam, May 1940, and converted to depot ship for U-boat crews at Gdynia. Recovered at Kiel in damaged condition and refitted 1945; resumed passenger service January 1947. Broken up Baltimore 1953.

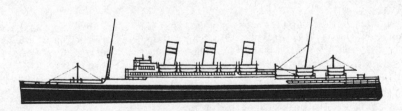

212 STATENDAM (III)

'29, (1929-40) 29,511. 697 x 81. Twin screw, turbines, 19 knots. Laid down 1921 by Harland & Wolff, Belfast. Work suspended for time due to U.S. Immigration restrictions. Hull towed to Rotterdam 1927 for completion at Wilton-Fijenoord yard; M.V. Rotterdam-New York, 11 April 1929. Laid up at Rotterdam at outbreak of war, September 1939. Destroyed by fire in fighting around docks during German invasion of Netherlands, May 1940; broken up later in year.

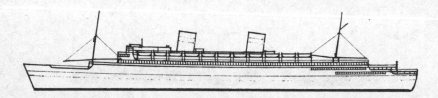

213 NIEUW AMSTERDAM (II) ●

'38, (1938-　) 36,982. 759 x 88. Twin screw, turbines, 21 knots. Built by Rotterdamsche Droogdok Maatschappij, Rotterdam. The largest ship built to date in the Netherlands. M.V. Rotterdam-New York, 10 May 1938. Laid up at New York 1939. Refitted and armed at Halifax 1940; converted to troopship at Singapore 1941. During World War II transported 378,361 passengers and logged 530,452 miles, returning to Rotterdam on 10 April 1946 for the first time in nearly seven years. Extensively rebuilt; returned to passenger service, 29 October 1947. One of the most famous transatlantic liners ever built.

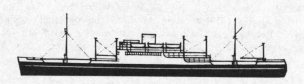

214 NOORDAM (II)

'38, (1938-63). 10,726. 502 x 64. Twin screw, motorship, 17 knots. Built by P. Smit Jun., Rotterdam. M.V. Rotterdam-New York, 28 September 1938. Served as troopship in World War II; re-entered passenger service July 1946. Sold to Cielomar Steamship Corp. (Panama) 1963. Chartered to Cie. des Messageries Maritimes; renamed OCEANIEN. Broken up Split, Yugoslavia, 1967.

215 ZAANDAM

'39, (1939-42) 10,909. Details as (214). Built by Wilton-Fijenoord, Schiedam. M.V. Rotterdam-New York, 7 January 1939. Torpedoed and sunk off the coast of Brazil, 2 November 1942, with loss of 130 lives. Three members of ships company survived 83 days drifting on a raft.

216 WESTERDAM

'46, (1946-65) 12,149. 518 x 66. Twin screw, motorship, 18 knots. Laid down September 1939 by Wilton-Fijenoord. Construction continued under German occupation. Sunk three times by Dutch underground to prevent use by Germans. Finally completed after war; M.V. Rotterdam-New York, 1 July 1946. Broken up Alicante, Spain, 1965.

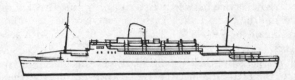

217 RYNDAM ●
'51, (1951-   ) 15,015. 503 x 69. Single screw, turbines, 16 knots. Laid down as freighter DINTELDYK by Wilton-Fijenoord; design changed during construction. M.V. Rotterdam-New York, 16 July 1951. Transferred to Europe-Canada Line 1966; placed on world cruise service as school ship. Transferred to Trans-Ocean Steamship Co 1967 for summer transatlantic student tourist service; renamed WATERMAN. Returned to Holland-America Line October 1968; renamed RYNDAM.

218 MAASDAM (IV)
'52, (1952-68) 15,024. Details as (217). Built by Wilton-Fijenoord. M.V. Rotterdam-New York, 11 August 1952. Sold to Gdynia-America Line 1968; renamed STEFAN BATORY (269).

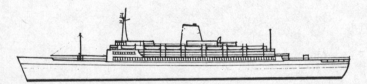

219 STATENDAM (IV) ●
'57, (1957-   ) 24,294. 643 x 79. Twin screw, turbines, 20 knots. Built by Wilton-Fijenoord, Schiedam. M.V. Rotterdam-New York, 6 February 1957.

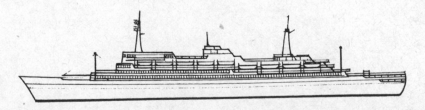

220 ROTTERDAM (V) ●
'59, (1959-   ) 38,645. 749 x 94. Twin screw, turbines, 20 knots. Built by Rotterdamsche Droogdok Maatschappij, Rotterdam. M.V. Rotterdam-New York, 3 September 1959. Flagship of the Holland-America Line fleet.

ORANJE LINE, ROTTERDAM (1953-1964)

The Maatschappij Zeetransport N.V., known as the Oranje Line, was established in 1937 to provide freight service between western European ports and St John, N.B., Quebec, Montreal and the Great Lakes. Passenger service was begun in September 1953 with the sailing of the PRINS WILLEM VAN ORANJE with accommodation for sixty passengers.

Six years later a larger ship, the PRINSES IRENE, was placed in service, followed by a running mate, the PRINSES MARGRIET. However, in 1964 the Company decided to withdraw from the passenger trade and disposed of the three vessels.

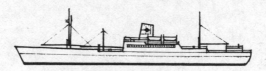

221 PRINSES IRENE
'59, (1959-64) 8,533. 456 x 61. Single screw, motorship, 16 knots. Built by De Merwede, Hardinxveld. 115 passengers in one class. M.V. Rotterdam-Montreal, 29 April, 1959. Sold to Verolme United Shipyards 1964. Resold to Republik Indonesia 1965; renamed TJUT NJAK DHIEN.

222 PRINSES MARGRIET
'61, (1961-67) 9,341. 456 x 61. Single screw, motorship, 17 knots. Built by De Merwede. 111 passengers in one class. M.V. Rotterdam-Montreal, 15 July 1961. Sold to Holland-America Line 1964. Chartered to Royal Netherlands Steamship Co (Netherlands) for West Indies service 1967. Sold to Republic of Nauru 1970; renamed ENNA G.

7 GREECE

NATIONAL STEAM NAVIGATION CO OF GREECE, PIRAEUS (1909-35)

The National Steam Navigation Co was founded by the Embiricos Brothers, whose first sailing from Patras to New York was made by the PATRIS on 2 April 1909. Four years later the Company purchased a number of second-hand vessels and placed orders in England for two new ships. Construction on the latter was halted by the war while three of the recently acquired ships were lost at sea.

At the end of the war, the new MEGALI HELLAS was delivered, her sister having been taken over by the British Government, completed in 1917, and torpedoed a year later. A British registered subsidiary, the Byron Line, was formed to purchase ex-German liners from the British Government. The first of these, the CLEVELAND, was soon resold. A second, the BREMEN, was renamed CONSTANTINOPLE, later KING ALEXANDER. Other purchases included the Orient Line's OMAR and the Anchor liner COLUMBIA, which were renamed EDISON and MOREAS. With the added tonnage, the Company's emigrant services were extended to the major ports of the Levant.

Increasing obsolesence and the loss of trade due to American immigration restrictions began to have serious financial effects and in 1928-29 all the British flagships were transferred to the National Steam Navigation Co. With the sale of the EDISON in 1935, the Company ceased to exist.

223 BYRON
'20, (1924-37) 9,272. 470(R) x 58. Twin screw, quadruple expansion engines, 17 knots. Launched
1914 by Cammell Laird & Co, Birkenhead, as VASILEFS CONSTANTINOS. Construction
suspended during war; renamed MEGALI HELLAS before completion. F.V. Piraeus-New York
1920. Transferred to subsidiary, Byron Steamship Co (Great Britain) for purposes of convenience
1924; renamed BYRON. Reverted to National Steam Navigation Co 1928. Broken up Italy 1937.

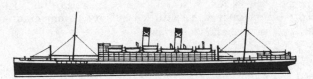

224 EDISON
'96, (1924-35) 11,103. 546 x 60. Twin screw, quadruple expansion engines, 15 knots. Built by
A.G. Vulkan, Stettin as KONIGIN LUISE for Norddeutscher Lloyd. Turned over to British
Government as war reparation. Bought by Orient Line (Great Britain) 1920; renamed OMAR.
Bought by Byron Steamship Co 1924; renamed EDISON. Transferred to National Steam Navigation
Co 1929. Broken up Italy 1935.

225 MOREAS
'02, (1926-29) 8,497. Formerly COLUMBIA (31) Anchor Line. Bought by Byron Steamship Co
1926; renamed MOREAS. Transferred to National Steam Navigation Co 1928. Broken up Italy
1929.

GREEK LINE, PIRAEUS (1939-)

The General Steam Navigation Co of Greece, known as the Greek Line, began operations in 1939 by buying the Anchor liner TUSCANIA, which was renamed NEA HELLAS and placed in service between Piraeus and New York. With the outbreak of war a few months later, the service was halted and, after the invasion of Greece in 1940, the NEA HELLAS was converted to serve as a troopship under British management until she was returned to the Company in 1947.

Immediately after the war the Company purchased three additional vessels of rather advanced age, registered them in Panama, and opened a service between Bremen and Montreal in 1950, shifting to New York a year later. In 1953 the Company commissioned its first and only new ship, the OLYMPIA, which was registered until 1968 in Liberia

In the middle 1950s the two eldest ships, the COLUMBIA and CANBERRA were sold, while the NEPTUNIA ran aground in 1957 and was broken up. The following year the Company purchased the British emigrant ship NEW AUSTRALIA and renamed her ARKADIA to replace the NEW YORK, as the NEA HELLAS had been renamed.

In 1964 a much newer vessel, the Canadian Pacific's EMPRESS OF BRITAIN, was bought and renamed QUEEN ANNA MARIA. Since the sale of the ARKADIA in 1966, the Line's two modern liners have carried on a programme of cruising and transatlantic service from eastern Mediterranean ports.

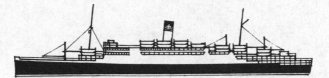

226 NEW YORK
'22, (1939-61) 16,991. Formerly TUSCANIA (33) Anchor Line. Bought by Greek Line 1939;
renamed NEA HELLAS. F.V. Piraeus-New York, 19 May 1939. Converted to serve as British
troopship under Anchor Line management 1940-46. Reverted to Greek Line, refitted and
resumed passenger service August 1947. Renamed NEW YORK 1955. Laid up at Piraeus,
November 1959; broken up Onimichi, Japan 1961.

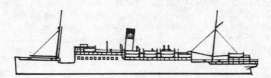

227 COLUMBIA
'13, (1946-57) 9,424. 466 x 60. Triple screw, combination triple expansion engines and turbine,
15 knots. Built by Harland & Wolff, Belfast, as KATOOMBA for McIlwraith & McEachern & Co
(Australia). Operated in Sydney-Fremantle service. Served as troopship in both World Wars. Bought
by Greek Line 1946; registered in Panama. F.V. Piraeus-New York, 1946. Refitted 1949; renamed
COLUMBIA. Laid up at Piraeus, November 1957; broken up Nagasaki 1958.

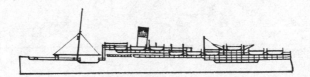

228 NEPTUNIA
'20, (1949-58) 10,474. 506(R) x 59. Twin screw, triple expansion engines, 16 knots. Built by
Nederlandsche Dok en Scheepsbouw, Amsterdam as JOHAN DE WITT for Nederland Line
(Netherlands). Lengthened by 24 feet 1935. Bought by Greek Line 1948; renamed NEPTUNIA
and registered in Panama. Extensively refitted; after funnel and mainmast removed. F.V. Piraeus-
New York, 1949. Beached in sinking condition near Cobh, Ireland after grounding 2 November
1957. Towed to Rotterdam for breaking up 1958.

229 CANBERRA
'13, (1949-54) 7,707. 426 x 57. Twin screw, quadruple expansion engines, 15 knots. Built by
Alexander Stephen & Sons, Linthouse, Glasgow for Australian Steamships Pty. Ltd (Australia);
operated in Queensland coastal trade. Served as troopship 1917-19. Bought by Greek Line 1948;
registered in Panama. F.V. Piraeus-New York, 1949. Sold to Dominican Government 1954; renamed
ESPANA. Broken up Dominican Republic 1959.

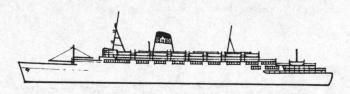

230 OLYMPIA ●
'53, (1953-   ) 17,269. 611 x 79. Twin screw, turbines, 21 knots. Built by Alexander Stephen &
Sons, Linthouse, Glasgow: the first ship built for the Greek Line. Registered in Liberia. M.V.
Southampton-New York, 20 October 1953. Registry transferred to Greece 1968.

116

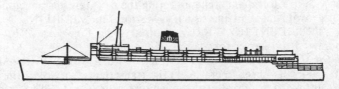

231 ARKADIA
'31, (1958-66) 20,650. 590 x 76. Quadruple screw, turbo-electric, 19 knots. Built by Vickers-Armstrongs, Newcastle, as MONARCH OF BERMUDA for Furness Bermuda Line (Great Britain). Served as troopship in World War II. Gutted by fire while being reconditioned for passenger service 24 March 1947. Bought by British Ministry of Transport 1948 and extensively refitted; three funnels reduced to one. Placed in Australian emigrant service under management of Shaw Savill Line (Great Britain) 1950; renamed NEW AUSTRALIA. Bought by Greek Line 1958; renamed ARKADIA. F.V. Bremen-Montreal, 22 May 1958. Broken up Valencia 1966.

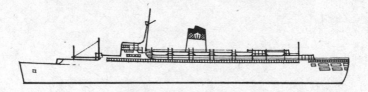

232 QUEEN ANNA MARIA ●
'56, (1965-) 21,716. Formerly EMPRESS OF BRITAIN (89) Canadian Pacific. Bought by Greek Line November 1964 and refitted at Genoa; renamed QUEEN ANNA MARIA. F.V. Piraeus-New York, 24 March 1965.

CHANDRIS LINE, PIRAEUS (1966-)

In 1959 the Chandris Group of steamship companies embarked on a programme of buying ships and refitting them for cruising service in the Mediterranean, as well as for emigrant service to Australia. Purchases during the next few years included a number of well known American liners such as Matson Line's LURLINE, American President Line's PRESIDENT HOOVER and United States Line's AMERICA which had been withdrawn from service for reasons of economy.

In 1966 the Company bought the QUEEN FREDERICA (originally the Matson liner MALOLO) which had been operating in the transatlantic service of the National Hellenic American Line. Two years later, the Union-Castle liner KENYA CASTLE was purchased and renamed AMERIKANIS. Both of these ships, after a few transatlantic voyages, engaged primarily in cruising.

Two more large ships were purchased early in 1970: the American President Line's PRESIDENT ROOSEVELT and the Cogedar Line's AURELIA. In the same year, the ELLINIS, formerly the LURLINE, which had been in the Australian service, was transferred to round-the-world cruising with calls at New York and Southampton, making a return western voyage during the summer.

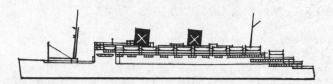

233 QUEEN FREDERICA ●

'27, (1955-66) 21,239. Formerly ATLANTIC (275) Home Lines. Transferred to Greek flag subsidiary, National Hellenic American Line 1954; renamed QUEEN FREDERICA. Registered as VASILESSA FREIDERIKI. F.V. Piraeus-New York, 29 January 1955. Bought by Chandris Line 1966; placed on Australian service later in year. Chartered to Sovereign Cruises 1968.

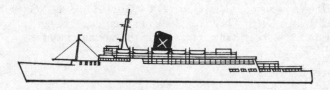

234 AMERIKANIS ●

'52, (1968-   ) 19,904. 577 x 74. Twin screw, turbines, 19 knots. Built by Harland & Wolff, Belfast, as KENYA CASTLE for Union-Castle Line (Great Britain); operated on South African service. Bought by Chandris Lines and extensively refitted 1968; renamed AMERIKANIS. F.V. Piraeus-New York, 8 August 1968.

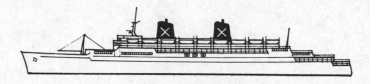

235 ELLINIS ●

'32, (1970-   ) 24,351. 642 x 79. Twin screw, turbines, 20 knots. Built by Bethlehem Shipbuilding Corp., Quincy, Massachusetts, as LURLINE for Matson Line (United States); operated on California-Hawaii service. Served as troopship in Pacific in World War II; resumed passenger service 1948. Bought by Chandris Lines and extensively refitted 1963; renamed ELLINIS. Placed in United Kingdom-Australia service. Transferred to round-the-world service 1970, making three eastbound and one westbound Atlantic crossings during the summer season.

8 SWEDEN

SWEDISH AMERICAN LINE, GOTHENBURG (1915-)

The Rederiaktiebolaget Sverige-Nordamerika was established in November 1914 to operate a shipping service between Gothenburg and New York. Despite the difficulties of obtaining a suitable ship during World War I, the POTSDAM was purchased from the Holland-America Line, renamed STOCKHOLM, and sailed from Gothenburg on 11 December 1915 to open the service.

Due to wartime conditions, the one-ship service under a neutral flag, though infrequent, proved highly profitable. After the war the company, renamed A/B Svenska Amerika Linien in 1925, acquired two additional vessels by purchase and charter. The first new construction was the GRIPSHOLM, built in 1925, followed by the KUNGSHOLM (II) in 1928.

The Line suffered a series of setbacks when the STOCKHOLM (II) was destroyed by fire in 1938 while fitting out at Trieste and her replacement STOCKHOLM (III) was sunk during the war. STOCKHOLM (IV), built in 1948, collided with and sank the Italian liner ANDREA DORIA in 1956.

Today the Line's two modern liners, the GRIPSHOLM and KUNGSHOLM, are engaged primarily in a varied schedule of long-range cruises throughout the year interspersed with a few transatlantic crossings in the summer months.

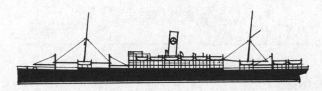

236 STOCKHOLM (I)

'00, (1915-28) 12,606. 570 x 62. Twin screw, triple expansion engines, 15 knots. Built by Blohm & Voss, Hamburg, as POTSDAM for Holland-America Line. Bought by Swedish American Line 1915; renamed STOCKHOLM. F.V. Gothenburg-New York, 11 December 1915. Sold to A/S Thor Dahl (Norway) for conversion to whaling factory 1928; renamed SOLGLIMT. Captured by Germans auxiliary cruiser PINGUIN in Antarctic, 14 January 1941; sent home as prize. Scuttled as blockship in Cherbourg harbour, 29 June 1944. Raised and broken up 1947.

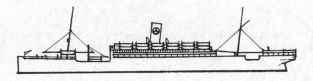

237 DROTTNINGHOLM

'05, (1920-48) 11,182. 538 x 60. Triple screw, turbines, 18 knots. Built by Alexander Stephen & Sons, Linthouse, Glasgow, as VIRGINIAN for Allan Line (Great Britain). Commissioned as armed merchant cruiser in 10th Cruiser Squadron December 1914. Transferred to Canadian Pacific 1917. Bought by Swedish American Line 1920; renamed DROTTNINGHOLM. F.V. Gothenburg-New York, May 1920. Famous as "mercy" ship during World War II, carrying exchanged prisoners of war and internees under the auspices of the Red Cross. Resumed passenger service March 1946; the oldest liner in the Atlantic trade. Sold to Home Lines 1948 for South American service; renamed BRASIL. Renamed HOMELAND (277) 1951.

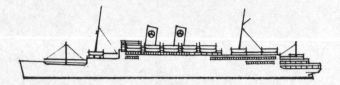

238 GRIPSHOLM (I)
'25, (1925-54) 18,815. 587 x 74. Twin screw, motorship, 17 knots. Built by Sir W.G. Armstrong, Whitworth & Co, Newcastle. M.V. Gothenburg-New York, 21 November 1925. The first diesel-engined transatlantic liner. Served as Red Cross repatriation ship during war. Resumed passenger service March 1946. Extensively refitted with new funnels and longer bow at Kiel 1950. Sold to Norddeutscher Lloyd 1954; renamed BERLIN (175) 1955.

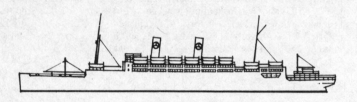

239 KUNGSHOLM (II)
'28, (1928-42) 21,532. 609 x 78. Twin screw, motorship, 17 knots. Built by Blohm & Voss. M.V. Gothenburg-New York, 24 November 1928. Extensively employed in winter cruising. Requisitioned by United States Government for service as troopship December 1941; renamed JOHN ERICCSON. Seriously damaged by fire at New York, March 1947. Repurchased by Swedish American Line and refitted at Genoa. Sold to Home Lines (Panama) 1948; renamed ITALIA (276).

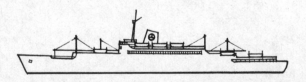

240 STOCKHOLM (IV)
'48, (1948-60) 12,396. 525 x 69. Twin screw, motorship, 19 knots. Built by Gotaverken, Gothenburg; the largest passenger ship built in Sweden. M.V. Gothenburg-New York, 21 February 1948. Severely damaged in collision with Italian liner ANDREA DORIA (138) which sank off Nantucket Island, 26 July 1956. Returned to service in December of same year. Sold to V.E.B. Deutsche Seereederei (East Germany) 1960; renamed VOLKERFREUNDSCHAFT.

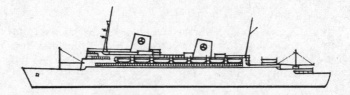

241   KUNGSHOLM (III)
'53, (1953-65) 21,164. 600 x 77. Twin screw, motorship, 19 knots. Built by De Schelde
Koninklijke Maatschappij, Flushing. M.V. Gothenburg-New York, 24 November 1953. Sold to
Norddeutscher Lloyd 1965; renamed EUROPA (177).

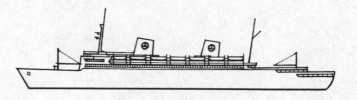

242   GRIPSHOLM (II) ●
'57, (1957-   ) 23,216. 631 x 82. Twin screw motorship, 19 knots. Built by S.A. Ansaldo, Sestri
Ponente. M.V. Gothenburg-New York, 14 May 1957.

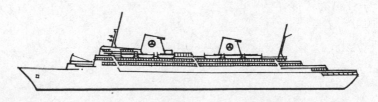

243   KUNGSHOLM (IV) ●
'66, (1966-   ) 26,677. 660 x 87. Twin screw, motorship, 21 knots. Built by John Brown & Co,
Clydebank, Glasgow. M.V. Gothenburg-New York, 24 April 1966.

9 NORWAY

NORWEGIAN AMERICA LINE, OSLO (1913-   )

Founded in 1910, the Norske Amerika Linje A/S placed contracts the following year for the construction of two ships for service between Oslo, Bergen and New York. Passenger service was inaugurated with the sailing of the KRISTIANIAFJORD from Christiania (Oslo) on 4 June 1913 followed by her sister, the BERGENSFJORD, three months later.

The KRISTIANIAFJORD was wrecked near Cape Race in July 1917 and for the next twenty years the service was carried on with the BERGENSFJORD and STAVANGERFJORD. In 1938 the OSLOFJORD joined the fleet only to be mined and sunk two years later while on war transport duty.

Post-war construction at regular intervals of three new liners of notable design has served to maintain the Line's fine reputation, both for cruising and for summer trans-atlantic service.

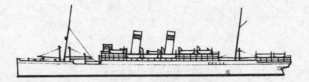

244 BERGENSFJORD (I)
'13, (1913-46) 11,013. 530 x 61. Twin screw, quadruple expansion engines, 16 knots. Built by
Cammell Laird & Co, Birkenhead. M.V. Christiania-New York, 27 September 1913. Continued
regular service throughout World War I. Left Norway shortly before German invasion in spring of
1940. Laid up at New York until November; refitted as allied troopship at Halifax the following
month. Returned to Norwegian America Line 1946. Sold to Home Lines 1946, renamed
ARGENTINA (278).

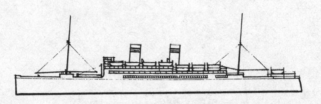

245 STAVANGERFJORD
'18, (1918-63) 14,015. 533 x 64. Twin screw, quadruple expansion engines, 16 knots. Built by
Cammell Laird & Co. M.V. Oslo-New York, November 1918. Laid up at Oslo, December 1939;
taken over by Germans as troop depot ship after invasion of Norway. Resumed passenger service
August 1945. Withdrawn from service December 1963 after forty five years of outstanding service,
having completed 770 Atlantic crossings, steamed almost 2,800,000 miles, and carried nearly a
half million passengers. Broken up Hong Kong 1964.

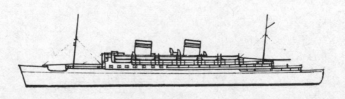

246 OSLOFJORD (I)
' 38, (1938-40) 18,673. 588 x 73. Twin screw, motorship, 19 knots. Built by A.G. Weser, Bremen.
M.V. Oslo-New York, 4 June 1938. Laid up New York early in 1940; taken over as Allied troopship
in October. Struck magnetic mine off Tynemouth, 13 December 1940; beached, but became a total
loss.

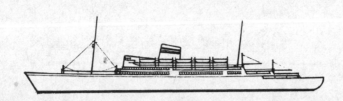

247 OSLOFJORD (II)

' 49, (1949-69) 16,844. 577 x 72. Twin screw, motorship, 20 knots. Built by Nederlandsche Dok en Scheepsbouw, Amsterdam. M.V. Oslo-New York, 26 November 1949. Chartered to Costa Line for cruising service 1969; renamed FULVIA. Caught fire after engine room explosion and sank 140 miles north of Canary Islands, 20 July 1970; all passengers and crew saved.

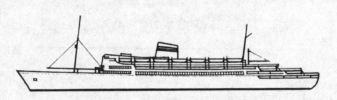

248 BERGENSFJORD (II) ●

'56, (1956-   ) 18,739. 578 x 72. Twin screw, motorship, 20 knots. Built by Swan, Hunter & Wigham Richardson, Wallsend-on-Tyne. M.V. Oslo-New York, 30 May 1956. Sold to Cie. Generale Transatlantique 1971; renamed DE GRASSE.

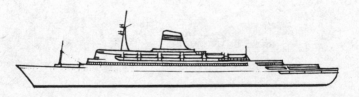

249 SAGAFJORD ●

'65, (1965-   ) 24,002. 620 x 82. Twin screw, motorship, 20 knots. Built by Soc. des Forges et Chantiers de la Mediterranee, La Seyne. M.V. Oslo-New York, 2 October 1965.

10 DENMARK

SCANDINAVIAN-AMERICAN LINE, COPENHAGEN (1902-1935)

In 1898, the old-established United Steamship Co of Copenhagen took over the Thingvalla Line together with its four steamers. The company was renamed the Skandinavien-Amerika Linien to operate a service between Copenhagen and New York.

Three new ships were laid down, the first of which, the OSCAR II, made the initial sailing in March of 1902. Two years later, the Holland-America Line's ROTTERDAM was purchased and renamed C.F. TIETGEN. She was sold in 1913 to make way for the new FREDERIK VIII. Sailing under a neutral flag, all four of the Company's ships survived World War I.

The depression of the early 1930s caused a drastic reduction in passenger traffic and this, combined with the fact that three of the ships were nearly thirty years old, resulted in their withdrawal from service starting in 1931. The FREDERIK VIII was finally laid up in 1935 to end the Line's passenger service.

250 OSCAR II
'02, (1902-31) 10,012. 515 x 58. Twin screw, triple expansion engines, 16 knots. Built by Alexander Stephen & Sons, Linthouse, Glasgow. M.V. Copenhagen-New York,12 March 1902. Broken up England 1931.

251 HELLIG OLAV
'03, (1903-34) 9,939. Details as (250). Built by Alexander Stephen & Sons. M.V. Copenhagen-New York, 26 March 1903. Broken up Blyth 1934.

252 UNITED STATES
'03, (1903-34) 10,095. Details as (250). Built by Alexander Stephen & Sons. M.V. Copenhagen-New York, 3 June 1903. Broken up Leghorn, Italy 1935.

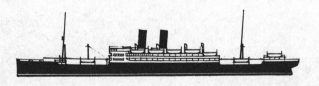

253 FREDERIK VIII
'14, (1914-35) 11,850. 544 x 62. Twin screw, triple expansion engines, 16 knots. Built by A.G. Vulkan, Stettin. M.V. Copenhagen-New York, 5 February 1914. Broken up Blyth 1937.

BALTIC AMERICAN LINE, COPENHAGEN (1921-1930)

At the end of World War I, the passenger ships RUSSIA, KURSK, CZAR and CZARITZA of the Russian American Line which had been sailing under British registry since the Russian Revolution, were returned to the East Asiatic Company (Det Ostasiatiske Kompagni), their former operators. The Company renamed them LATVIA, POLONIA, ESTONIA and LITUANIA respectively, and inaugurated a service between Libau and New York under the name Baltic American Line with the sailing of the POLONIA in January 1921.

The imposition of immigration quotas in the early 1920s resulted in the sale of the LATVIA and in 1930 the three remaining vessels were sold to the Polish Transatlantic Shipping Company to end the Line's existence.

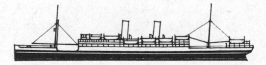

254 ESTONIA
'12, (1921-30) 6,503. 426(R) x 53. Twin screw, quadruple expansion engines, 16 knots. Built by Barclay, Curle & Co, Glasgow, as CZAR for Russian American Line. During Russian Revolution transferred to British registry under Cunard management 1917-18. Line re-organized as Baltic American Line 1921; renamed ESTONIA. F.V. Libau-New York, February 1921. Sold to Polish Transatlantic Shipping Co 1930; renamed PULASKI (264).

255 LITUANIA
'15, (1921-30) 6,598, 440(R) x 53. Twin screw, quadruple expansion engines, 15 knots. Built by Barclay, Curle & Co as CZARITZA for Russian American Line. Transferred to British registry 1917-18. Line re-organized as Baltic American Line 1921; renamed LITUANIA. F.V. Libau-New York, February 1921. Sold to Polish Transatlantic Shipping Co 1930; renamed KOSCIUSZKO (265).

11 SPAIN

COMPANIA TRASATLANTICA ESPANOLA, MADRID (1900-)

The Compania Trasatlantica was formed in 1881 to take over the shipping service between Spain and Cuba of A. Lopez y Cia. of Barcelona. However, it was not until 1900 that a through service to New York, Havana and Vera Cruz was established. In contrast to all other transatlantic shipping lines, no North American port was the terminal; the ships continued on to Cuba and Mexico.

During World War I, the Company earned large profits and was thus able to order the construction of six new ships and to dispose of a large number of older vessels, most of which had been in service for over thirty years.

The outbreak of the Spanish Civil War in 1936 completely disrupted the Company's services and in the ensuing fighting a number of its ships were sunk, interned or damaged. Sailings were not resumed until 1939.

In 1953 two new motorships, the GUADALUPE and COVADONGA, were placed in commission and carry on the transatlantic services of the Company.

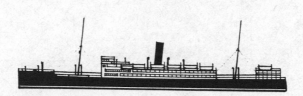

256 CRISTOBAL COLON
'23, (1923-36) 10,833. 499(R) x 61. Twin screw, turbines, 16 knots. Built by Soc. Espanola de
Construccion Naval, Ferrol. Homeward bound at outbreak of Spanish Civil War, she was diverted
to St Nazaire, seized by Nationalist members of crew, and sailed for Mexico. Wrecked near Bermuda
24 October 1936.

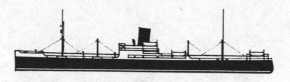

257 HABANA
'23, (1923-37) (1947-60) 10,551. 500 x 61. Twin screw, turbines, 16 knots. Built by Soc. Espanola
de Construccion Naval, Bilbao, as ALFONSO XIII. Renamed HABANA upon King's abdication
1931. Laid up at Barcelona at start of Civil War. Gutted by fire during refit at Bilbao 1937; bulk of
superstructure removed and rebuilt as cargo ship 1940. Reduced passenger accommodation
reinstalled at Brooklyn, New York 1947. Withdrawn from service 1960. Bought by Pescanova
S.A. (Spain) and converted to fish factory 1962; renamed GALICIA.

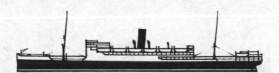

258 JUAN SEBASTIAN ELCANO
'28, (1928-37) 9,965. 467 x 56. Twin screw, turbines, 16 knots. Built by Soc. Espanola de Construccion Naval, Bilbao. Seized by Russian forces in Black Sea at end of Civil War and assigned to Soviet Navy 1939; renamed VOLGA.

259 MAGALLANES
'28, (1928-53) 9,689. Details as (258). Built by Soc. Espanola de Construccion Naval, Cadiz. Collided with and sank, Italian steamer in Dardanelles, June 1937, while enroute to Russia to load munitions for use in Civil War. Resumed passenger service 1940. Reconstructed with single funnel 1941. Transferred to Cuba-Mexico service 1953. Laid up at Bilbao 1954; broken up 1957.

260 MARQUES DE COMILLAS
'28, (1928-53) 9,922. Details as (258). Built by Soc. Espanola Construccion, Ferrol. M.V. Cadiz-New York, November 1928. Resumed sailings after Civil War late 1939. Reconstructed with single funnel 1941. Transferred to Cuba-Mexico service 1953. Gutted by fire in yard at Ferrol, 6 November 1961; broken up Bilbao 1962.

261 GUADALUPE ●
'53, (1953-) 10,226. 487 x 67. Single screw, motorship, 17 knots. Launched October 1951 as cargo liner MONASTERIO DE GUADALUPE by Soc. Espanola de Construccion Naval, Bilbao, for Empresa Nacional Elcano (Spain). Bought by Cia. Trasatlantica Espanola during construction and completed to modified design; renamed GUADALUPE. M.V. Bilbao-New York, 21 March 1953.

262 COVADONGA ●
'53, (1953-) 10,226. Details as (261). Launched May 1951 as cargo liner MONASTERIO DE LA RABIDA by Cia. Euskalduna, Bilbao, for Empreso Nacional Elcano. Bought by Cia. Trasatlantica Espanola during construction; renamed COVADONGA. M.V. Bilbao-New York, 27 August 1953.

12 POLAND

GDYNIA-AMERICA LINE, GDYNIA (1930-51) (1957-)

The Polish Transatlantic Shipping Co Ltd was established in 1930 to take over the transatlantic service of the three ships of the Baltic American Line. These ships the POLONIA, ESTONIA and LITUANIA were transferred from Danish to Polish registry and the ESTONIA and LITUANIA were renamed PULASKI and KOSCIUSZKO. The first sailing from Gdynia to Copenhagen, Halifax and New York took place in March 1930.

Four years later two new ships, the PILSUDSKI and BATORY were ordered under a trade agreement with Italy, and shortly afterward the name of the Line was changed to Gdynia-Amerika Linje Zeglugowe Spolka. Upon the entry of these ships into service, the older ships were transferred to a new South American service.

All ships of the Line served with the Allied forces in World War II, during which the PILSUDSKI was sunk. After the war, the SOBIESKI sailed for a time between Italy and New York, while the BATORY operated on the Gdynia-New York run until being barred from New York docking facilities in 1951. The service was revived in 1957 with Montreal as the western terminal.

In 1969, the BATORY was retired and the former Holland-America liner MAASDAM was purchased, extensively remodelled and renamed STEPHAN BATORY to carry on the Line's transatlantic service.

263 POLONIA
'10, (1930-36) 7,890. 450(R) x 56. Twin screw, quadruple expansion engines, 16 knots. Built by Barclay, Curle & Co, Glasgow, as KURSK for Russian American Line (Russia). Transferred to British registry during Russian Revolution 1917-18. Line reorganized as Baltic American Line 1921; renamed POLONIA. Bought by Polish Transatlantic Shipping Co 1930. Line renamed Gdynia-America Line 1935. Transferred to South American service 1936. Broken up Italy 1939.

264 PULASKI
'12, (1930-36) 6,503. Formerly ESTONIA (254) Baltic American Line. Bought by Polish Trans-atlantic Shipping Co 1930; renamed PULASKI. Transferred to South American service 1936. Converted to allied troopship 1939. Bought by British Ministry of Transport 1946; renamed EMPIRE PENRYN. Broken up Blyth 1949.

265 KOSCIUSZKO
'15, (1930-36) 6,598. Formerly LITUANIA (255) Baltic American Line. Bought by Polish Trans-atlantic Shipping Co 1930; renamed KOSCIUSZKO. Transferred to South American service 1936. Commissioned as depot ship in Polish Navy 1939; renamed GDYNIA. Bought by British Ministry of Transport 1946; renamed EMPIRE HELFORD. Broken up Germany 1950.

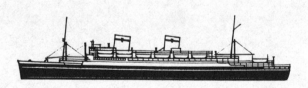

266 PILSUDSKI
'35, (1935-39) 14,294. 526 x 70. Twin screw, motorship, 18 knots. Built by Cantieri Riunite dell' Adriatica, Monfalcone. M.V. Gdynia-New York, September 1935. Commissioned as armed merchant cruiser 1939. Torpedoed and sunk off the mouth of the Humber River, 26 November 1939.

267 BATORY
'36, (1936-51) (1957-69) 14,287. Details as (266). Built by Cantieri Riuniti dell' Adriatico. M.V. Gdynia-New York, 18 May 1936. Converted to Allied troopship 1939; resumed passenger service May 1947. Involved in several political incidents which resulted in denial of entry to the Port of New York 1951; transferred to Gdynia-Bombay, Karachi service. Returned to transatlantic service 1957. Converted to floating hotel at Gdansk 1969. Broken up Hong Kong 1971.

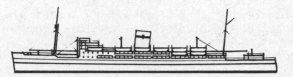

268 SOBIESKI
'39, (1946-50) 11,030. 511 x 67. Twin screw, motorship, 17 knots. Built by Swan, Hunter &
Wigham Richardson, Newcastle for Gdynia-South America service. Converted to Allied troopship
1939. F.V. Italy-New York, 1946. Bought by Soviet Union 1950; renamed GRUZIA.

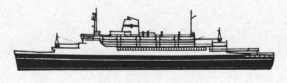

269 STEFAN BATORY ●
'52, (1969-   ) 15,024. Formerly MAASDAM (218) Holland-America Line. Bought by Gdynia-
America Line and extensively remodelled 1968; renamed STEFAN BATORY. F.V. Gdynia-Montreal
11 April 1969.

13 ISRAEL

ZIM LINES, HAIFA (1953-1967)

The Zim Israel Navigation Co Ltd was formed in 1945 to establish a Mediterranean service to carry Jewish emigrants from Europe to Palestine at a time when international recognition had yet to be accorded to the new state of Israel. To do so, it was forced to acquire whatever tonnage was available on the market.

In 1953, the forty year old ARGENTINA was purchased from the Home Lines and renamed JERUSALEM. On 29 April 1953 she inaugurated a transatlantic service from Haifa to New York. Two years later the new ships ISRAEL and ZION, built in Hamburg under the Israeli-German Reparation Agreement, began a schedule of regular departures. Three additional ships were built for Mediterranean service as well as for occasional voyages to South America and cruising. The Line's handsome flagship SHALOM was added in 1964.

In December of 1965 however, the Company announced its withdrawal from transatlantic service and the three ships involved were sold during the course of the next two years.

270 JERUSALEM
'13, (1953-55) 11,015. Formerly ARGENTINA (278) Home Line. Bought by Zim Lines 1953; renamed JERUSALEM F.V. Haifa-New York, 29 April 1953. Transferred to Haifa-Marseilles service 1955. Renamed ALIYA 1957. Broken up La Spezia 1959.

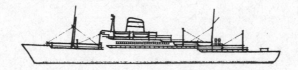

271 ISRAEL
'55, (1955-66) 9,831. 501 x 65. Single screw, turbines, 18 knots. Built by Deutsche Werft A.G. Hamburg, as reparation for Jewish losses during World War II. F.V. Haifa-New York, 13 October 1955. Sold to Empresa Insulana de Navegacao (Portugal) 1966; renamed ANGRA DO HEROISMO.

272 ZION
'56, (1956-66) 9,855. Details as (271). Built by Deutsche Werft A.G. F.V. Haifa-New York 9 March 1956. Sold to Sociedade Geral (Portugal) 1966; renamed AMELIA DE MELLO.

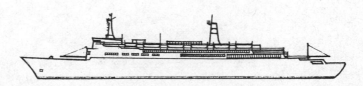

273 SHALOM
'64, (1964-67) 25,320. 628 x 82. Twin screw, turbines, 20 knots. Built by Chantiers de l'Atlantique (Penhoet-Loire) St Nazaire. M.V. Haifa-New York, 16 April 1964. Rammed the Norwegian tanker STOLT DAGALI, 26 November 1964 while outward bound from New York on a West Indies cruise. Stern section of the tanker sank with loss of 19 lives. Sold to German Atlantic Line 1967; renamed HANSEATIC (183).

14 SOVIET UNION

BALTIC STEAMSHIP LINE, LENINGRAD (1966-)

At the end of World War II, the shipping and yards of the Soviet Union, as well as the Central European areas under its control, were devastated by the ravages of invading armies and aerial bombing attacks. The immediate post-war shipping requirements were met by the acquisition of most of the surviving German merchant fleet, including the salvaging of sunken ships in Baltic waters. Faced with the necessity of restoring wrecked facilities and at the same time creating a modern submarine fleet, merchant vessels were ordered abroad and it was not until the late 1950s that the new ships, built almost exclusively in satellite countries, began to come into service.

The Soviet merchant fleet, under the control of Sovtorgflot, is divided into four geographical areas. The Baltic Steamship Line, as its name implies, controls shipping in the Baltic Sea and operates a Leningrad-London service. On 13 April 1966, the Line opened a new transatlantic service between Leningrad and Montreal with the sailing of the ALEXANDR PUSHKIN. The service has continued during the summer months each year.

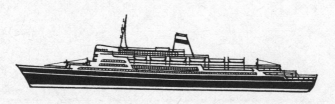

274 ALEXANDR PUSHKIN ●
'65, (1966-) 19,861. 578 x 78. Twin screw, motorship, 20 knots. Built by V.E.B. Mathias-Thesen Werft, Wismar, East Germany. The second of a class of five ships. F.V. Leningrad-Montreal 13 April 1966.

15 PANAMA AND LIBERIA

HOME LINES, GENOA (1949-)

The Home Lines began operations in 1946 by purchasing the Norwegian America liner BERGENSFJORD which was renamed ARGENTINA, registered in Panama, and placed in service to South America the following year. In the next two years the Line acquired three more ships; the Swedish American liners DROTTNINGHOLM and JOHN ERICCSON, and Matson Line's MATSONIA, which were renamed BRASIL, ITALIA and ATLANTIC.

Due to a falling off in the South American post-war boom, it was decided to inaugurate a service to New York. Accordingly, the ATLANTIC made the first sailing from Genoa on 14 May 1949, followed a month later by the ITALIA. Within a year the Line had completely withdrawn from the South American trade.

In 1951 the BRASIL was renamed HOMELAND and began a new Hamburg-New York service. In the next few years the ARGENTINA was sold; another Matson liner, the MARIPOSA was purchased and renamed HOMERIC; the ATLANTIC was transferred to a Greek flag subsidiary and renamed QUEEN FREDERICA; and the ancient HOMELAND was sold for breaking up.

Due to the decreasing transatlantic passenger traffic in the early 1960s, the two remaining ships the ITALIA and HOMERIC, were assigned to cruising to the West Indies from New York. In 1964 the ITALIA was sold for use as a floating hotel in the Bahamas and the following year the Line's finest ship, the luxurious OCEANIC was commissioned to join the HOMERIC in the Caribbean service.

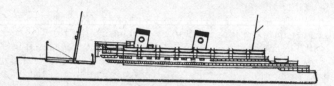

275 ATLANTIC

'27, (1949-54) 20,553. 582 x 83. Twin screw, turbines, 22 knots. Built by Wm Cramp & Sons Shipbuilding Co, Philadelphia, as MALOLO for Matson Line (United States). Renamed MATSONIA 1937. Served as troopship in Pacific 1941-45. Bought by Home Lines 1949; renamed ATLANTIC. F.V. Genoa-New York, 14 May 1949. Transferred to National Hellenic American Line (Greece) 1954; renamed QUEEN FREDERICA (233).

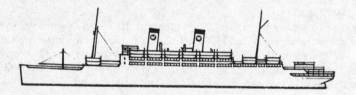

276 ITALIA

'28, (1949-61) 16,777. Formerly JOHN ERICCSON, ex KUNGSHOLM (239) Swedish American Line. Bought by Home Lines 1948; renamed ITALIA. Placed on Genoa-South America service. July 1948. Transferred to North Atlantic the following year; F.V. Genoa-New York, 12 June 1949. Transferred to New York-Nassau cruising service 1961. Sold to Freeport-Bahama Enterprises Ltd for use as floating hotel, Freeport 1964; renamed IMPERIAL BAHAMA. Broken up Bilbao 1965.

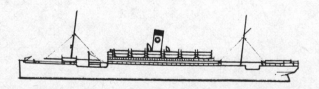

277 HOMELAND

'05, (1951-55) 10,249. Formerly DROTTNINGHOLM (237) Swedish American Line. Bought by Home Lines 1948; renamed BRASIL. Placed on Genoa-South America service, July 1948. Transferred to North Atlantic 1950. Renamed HOMELAND 1951; F.V. Hamburg-New York, 16 June 1951. Broken up Trieste 1955.

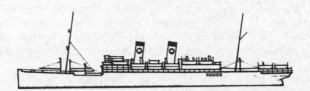

278 ARGENTINA
'13, (1952-53) 11,015. Formerly BERGENSFJORD (244) Norwegian America Line. Bought by
Home Lines 1946; renamed ARGENTINA. Placed on Genoa-South America service, January
1947. Transferred to North Atlantic 1952. Sold to Zim Lines 1953; renamed JERUSALEM (270).

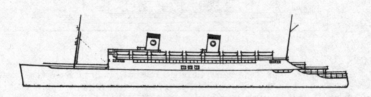

279 HOMERIC ●
'31, (1955-63) 18,563. 638 x 79. Twin screw, turbines, 20 knots. Built by Bethlehem Shipbuilding
Corp., Quincy, Massachusetts, as MARIPOSA for Matson Line (United States). Served as troopship
in World War II; afterward laid up at Alameda, California 1945-53. Bought by Home Lines 1954;
renamed HOMERIC and refitted at Trieste. F.V. Venice-New York, 24 January 1955. Transferred
to cruising service from New York to West Indies, October 1963.

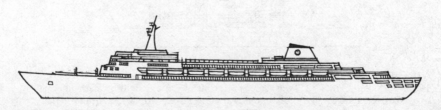

280 OCEANIC ●
'65, (1965-   ) 39,241. 782 x 97. Twin screw, turbines, 26 knots. Built by Cantieri Riunite dell'
Adriatico, Monfalcone. M.V. Genoa-New York, 3 April 1965. Regularly engaged in West Indies
cruising from New York.

INCRES LINE, NEW YORK (1950-51) (1960-   )

In 1950 the Incres Compania de Navegacion purchased the New Zealand Shipping
Co's liner RIMUTAKA. She was renamed EUROPA and registered in Panama, and
sailed from New York 5 July 1950 to open a new service to Antwerp. Fifteen months
later the transatlantic service was abandoned; the EUROPA was renamed NASSAU
and began a new service between New York and the Bahamas flying the Liberian
flag.

In 1958 the Line bought a second vessel, the Union-Castle Line's DUNNOTTAR
CASTLE, which was renamed VICTORIA and registered in Liberia. She was re-
engined and completely refitted as a modern cruise liner, and entered the Caribbean
service in 1960. Soon afterward the thirty eight year old NASSAU was sold. The
VICTORIA was purchased in 1964 by the Clipper Line of Malmo, Sweden but
continues to sail under the Incres Line name.

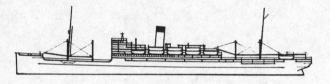

281 EUROPA
'23, (1950-51) 15,043. 573 x 72. Twin screw, turbines, 15 knots. Built by Sir W.G. Armstrong-
Whitworth & Co, Newcastle, as MONGOLIA for P & O Line (Great Britain). Transferred to
New Zealand Shipping Co (Great Britain) 1938; renamed RIMUTAKA. Bought by Incres Line
1950 and registry transferred to Panama; renamed EUROPA. F.V. New York-Antwerp, 5 July
1950. Withdrawn from transatlantic service October 1951; renamed NASSAU and registry
transferred to Liberia. Placed on New York-Nassau service. Sold to Cia. Naviera Turistica Mexicana
(Mexico) 1961; renamed ACAPULCO. Refitted at Glasgow and placed in Los Angeles-Acapulco
service 1962. Served as floating hotel at Seattle World's Fair later in the year. Laid up at Manzanillo
May 1963; towed to Japan and broken up Osaka 1964.

282 VICTORIA ●
'36, (1960-   ) 14,917. 573 x 72. Twin screw, motorship, 18 knots. Built by Harland & Wolff,
Belfast as DUNNOTTAR CASTLE for Union-Castle Line (Great Britain); on round-Africa service.
Commissioned as armed merchant cruiser 1939; converted to serve as troopship 1942-48. Resumed
passenger service February 1949. Bought by Incres Line 1958 and registry transferred to Liberia;
renamed VICTORIA. Extensively rebuilt and re-engined at Wilton-Fijnoord, Schiedam 1959. F.V.
Le Havre-New York, 8 January 1960. Placed on West Indies cruise service from New York with
periodic cruises to European waters.

AROSA LINE, GENEVA (1952-58)

Founded in 1952 as the Compania Internacional Transportadera of Panama, the Arosa Line was Swiss owned, with its ships based on Bremerhaven. The first sailing for Halifax via Zeebrugge and Southampton, was made on 18 March 1952 by the newly reconditioned AROSA KULM, built thirty two years before as the Hog Island troopship CANTIGNY.

During the next five years, three additional ships were purchased, modernised and refitted. They included the coastal passenger liner PUERTO RICO of the Bull Line, which was renamed AROSA STAR, and Messageries Maritime's FELIX ROUSSEL and LA MARSEILLAISE, renamed AROSA SUN and AROSA SKY respectively. In 1958 however, the Company experienced financial difficulties and was later declared bankrupt. The AROSA SKY was sold to the Costa Line, while the other three vessels were attached by customs officials to satisfy the demands of creditors and were eventually broken up or sold.

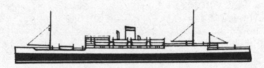

283 AROSA KULM
'20, (1952-59) 8,929. Formerly PROTEA, ex CITY OF ATHENS, ex VILLE D'ANVERS, ex AMERICAN BANKER (291) United States Lines. Bought by Arosa Line and completely refitted with greatly increased passenger capacity 1952; renamed AROSA KULM. F.V. Bremen-Halifax, 18 March 1952. Arrested for debt at Plymouth, England, December 1958. Broken up Ghent 1959.

284 AROSA STAR
'31, (1954-59) 9,070. 466 x 60. Single screw, turbines, 14 knots. Built by Bethlehem Shipbuilding Corp., Quincy, Massachusetts as BORINQUEN for New York & Porto Rico Line (United States). Served as troopship 1942-46. Bought by Bull Line (United States) 1949; renamed PUERTO RICO. Laid up at New York 1951. Bought by Arosa Line 1954; renamed AROSA STAR. F.V. Bremen-Quebec, May 1954. Seized for debt at Hamilton, Bermuda, December 1958. Sold to Eastern Steamship Lines (Panama) 1959; renamed BAHAMA STAR. Laid up at Jacksonville, Florida, November 1968. Sold for conversion to floating restaurant on West Coast 1969; renamed LA JENELLE. Dragged anchor in gale and drifted on beach at Port Hueneme, California 13 April 1970; broken up where she lay.

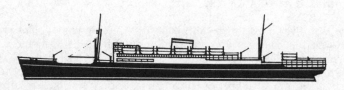

285 AROSA SUN

'30, (1955-60) 20,126. 597 x 68. Twin screw, motorship, 18 knots. Built by Ateliers et Chantiers de la Loire, St Nazaire, as FELIX ROUSSEL for Messageries Maritimes (France); sailed on Far East service. Confiscated by British Government after the fall of France, July 1940; resumed passenger service 1948. Bought by Arosa Line 1955; renamed AROSA SUN. F.V. Trieste-New York, 14 July 1955. Arrested for debt at Bremen, December 1958. Sold as floating hostel for factory workers at Ymuiden, Netherlands, September 1960.

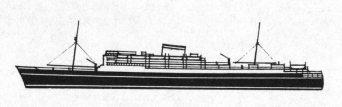

286 AROSA SKY

'39, (1957-58) 17,321. 594 x 75. Twin screw, motorship, 20 knots. Launched June 1944 by Soc. Provencale de Constructions Navales, La Ciotat, as MARECHAL PETAIN for Messageries Maritimes. Scuttled at Port de Bouc by retreating Germans 1945. Refloated, towed to La Ciotat and completed as LA MARSEILLAISE 1949. M.V. Marseilles-Far East, 18 August 1949. Bought by Arosa Line 1957; renamed AROSA SKY. F.V. Bremen-New York, 10 May 1957. Sold to Costa Line (Italy) 1958; renamed BIANCA C. Caught fire following explosion in engine room while lying at anchor at St George, Grenada, W.I., 22 October 1961; sank in deep water despite attempts to tow her to beach.

SHIPS NOT ILLUSTRATED

1 Cargo liners designed with limited passenger capacity.
2 Vessels built in the United States under emergency wartime shipbuilding programs and later fitted with a limited number of cabins for commercial sailings.
3 Standard "Victory" and other types of freighters fitted to carry tourist passengers and emigrants in dormitory accommodations.

GREAT BRITAIN

Canadian Pacific

287 BEAVERBRAE
'38, (1948-54) 9,034. 487 x 60. Single screw, diesel electric, 17 knots. Built by Blohm & Voss, Hamburg, as freighter HUASCARAN for Hamburg American Line. Ceded to Canadian Government as reparation. Bought by Canadian Pacific and refitted to carry 775 westbound emigrants 1947; renamed BEAVERBRAE. F.V. Bremen-Montreal, 25 February 1948. Sold to Cogedar Line (Italy) 1954; reconstructed and renamed AURELIA. Sold to Chandris Lines 1970; renamed ROMANZA.

Donaldson Line

288 LISMORIA
'45, (1948-66) 8,323. 455 x 62. Single screw, turbines, 15 knots. Built by Californian Shipbuilding Corp., Los Angeles, as cargo ship TAOS VICTORY. Bought by Donaldson Line and refitted to carry 55 passengers 1948; renamed LISMORIA. F.V. Glasgow-Montreal, 4 October 1948. Ceased carrying passengers 1966. Sold to Astroguardia Cia. Nav. (Panama) 1966; renamed NEON. Broken up Kaohsiung, Taiwan, 1967.

289 LAURENTIA
'45, (1949-66) 8,349. Details as (288). Built by Permanente Metals Corp., Richmond, California, as cargo ship MEDINA VICTORY. Bought by Donaldson Line 1948; renamed LAURENTIA. F.V. Glasgow-Montreal, 12 May 1949. Ceased carrying passengers 1966. Broken up Valencia 1967.

UNITED STATES

United States Lines

290 AMERICAN MERCHANT
'20, (1926-40) 7,430. 448 x 58. Single screw, turbines, 15 knots. Built by American International Shipbuilding Corp., Hog Island, Pennsylvania, as troopship AISNE for U.S. Shipping Board. Bought by American Merchant Lines (United States) and refitted to carry 80 passengers 1924; renamed AMERICAN MERCHANT. Transferred to United States Lines 1931. Sold to Antwerp Navigation Co (Belgium) 1940; renamed VILLE DE NAMUR. Torpedoed and sunk, June 1940.

291 AMERICAN BANKER
'20, (1926-40) 7,430. Details as (290). Built at Hog Island as CANTIGNY; renamed AMERICAN BANKER 1924. Transferred to United States Lines 1931. Sold to Antwerp Navigation Co 1940; renamed VILLE D'ANVERS. Sold to Isbrandtsen Line (Honduras) 1946; renamed CITY OF

ATHENS. Sold to Panamanian Lines (Panama) 1948; renamed PROTEA. Sold to Arosa Line 1952; renamed AROSA KULM (283).

292 AMERICAN FARMER
'20, (1926-40) 7,430. Details as (290). Built at Hog Island as OURCQ; renamed AMERICAN FARMER 1924. Transferred to United States Lines 1931. Sold to Antwerp Navigation Co 1940; renamed VILLE DE LIEGE. Torpedoed and sunk, April 1941.

293 AMERICAN SHIPPER
'21, (1926-40) 7,430. Details as (290). Built at Hog Island as TOURS; renamed AMERICAN SHIPPER 1924. Transferred to United States Lines 1931. Sold to Antwerp Navigation Co 1940; renamed VILLE DE MONS. Torpedoed and sunk. September 1940.

294 AMERICAN TRADER
'20, (1926-40) 7,430. Details as (290). Built at Hog Island as MARNE; renamed AMERICAN TRADER 1924. Transferred to United States Lines 1931. Sold to Antwerp Navigation Co 1940; renamed VILLE DE HASSELT. Torpedoed and sunk, August 1940.

295 AMERICAN IMPORTER
'20, (1931-40) 7,555. Details as (290). Built at Hog Island as SOMME; renamed AMERICAN IMPORTER 1924. Bought by United States Lines 1932. Sold to Antwerp Navigation Co 1940; renamed VILLE DE GAND. Torpedoed and sunk, August 1940.

296 AMERICAN TRAVELER
'20, (1931-40) 7,555. Details as (290) Built at Hog Island as CAMBRAI; renamed AMERICAN TRAVELER 1924. Bought by United States Lines 1932. Sold to Antwerp Navigation Co 1940; renamed VILLE D'ARLON. Torpedoed and sunk, December 1940.

297 MARINE FLASHER
'45, (1946-49) 12,558. 523 x 72. Single screw, turbines, 16 knots. Built as C-4 type troopship by Kaiser Co, Vancouver, Washington. Chartered by United States Lines; refitted to carry 550 tourist passengers on New York-Le Havre service 1946. Withdrawn from service 1949. Converted to container ship for Sea-Land Service (United States) 1966; renamed LONG BEACH.

298 MARINE PERCH
'45, (1946-48) 12,410. Details as (297). Built by Kaiser Co, Richmond, California. Chartered by United States Lines 1946-48. Converted to bulk carrier for Bulk Transport Inc. (United States) 1965; renamed YELLOWSTONE.

299 MARINE MARLIN
'45, (1946-48) 12,420. Details as (297). Built by Kaiser Co, Vancouver. Chartered by United States Lines 1946-48. Converted to cargo ship for Central Gulf Steamship Co,(United States) 1965; renamed GREEN BAY. Sunk by Viet Cong frogmen in Qui Nhon harbour, South Vietnam, 17 August 1971.

300 ERNIE PYLE
'45, (1946-47) 12,420. Details as (297). Built by Kaiser Co, Vancouver. Chartered by United States Lines 1946-47. Converted to cargo ship for Central Gulf Steamship Co 1965; renamed GREEN LAKE.

301 MARINE FALCON
'45, (1947-48) 12,420. Details as (297). Built by Kaiser Co, Vancouver. Chartered by United States Lines 1947-48. Converted to container ship for Sea-Land Service 1966; renamed TRENTON.

302 MARINE JUMPER
'45, (1947-48) 12,420. Details as (297). Built by Kaiser Co, Vancouver. Chartered by United States Lines 1947-48. Converted to container ship for Sea-Land Service 1966; renamed PANAMA.

303 MARINE TIGER
'45, (1947-49) 12,558. Details as (297). Built by Kaiser Co, Vancouver. Chartered by United States Lines 1947-49. Converted to container ship for Sea-Land service 1965; renamed OAKLAND.

304 MARINE SHARK
'45, (1948-49) 12,558. Details as (297). Built by Kaiser Co, Vancouver. Chartered by United States Lines 1948-49. Converted to container ship for Sea-Land Service 1968; renamed CHARLESTON.

Baltimore Mail Line, Baltimore

305 CITY OF BALTIMORE
'19, (1931-38) 8,424. 495 x 56. Single screw, turbines, 16 knots. Built by Bethlehem Shipbuilding Corp., Alameda, California, as STEADFAST for U.S. Shipping Board. Bought by Baltimore Mail Line; lengthened, re-engined and refitted to carry 80 passengers 1931. Renamed CITY OF BALTIMORE. F.V. Baltimore-Hamburg, 2 July 1931. Transferred to Panama Pacific Line (United States) 1938. Commissioned as U.S. Navy transport 1941; renamed U S S HEYWOOD (APA-6). Laid up in reserve fleet 1946.

306 CITY OF NORFOLK
'18, (1931-38) 8,424. Details as (305). Built by Bethlehem Shipbuilding Corp. as INDEPENDENCE. Bought by Baltimore Mail Line 1931; renamed CITY OF NORFOLK. Transferred to Panama Pacific Line 1938. Commissioned as transport 1941; renamed U S S NEVILLE (APA-9). Laid up in reserve fleet 1946.

307 CITY OF NEWPORT NEWS
'19, (1931-38) 8,424. Details as (305). Built by Bethlehem Shipbuilding Corp. as ARCHER. Bought by Baltimore Mail Line 1931; renamed CITY OF NEWPORT NEWS. Transferred to Panama Pacific Line 1938. Commissioned as transport 1941; renamed U S S FULLER (APA-7). Laid up in reserve fleet 1946.

308 CITY OF HAMBURG
'19, (1931-38) 8,424. Details as (305). Built by Bethlehem Shipbuilding Corp. as ECLIPSE. Bought by Baltimore Mail Line 1931; renamed CITY OF HAMBURG. Transferred to Panama Pacific Line 1938; renamed CITY OF SAN FRANCISCO. Commissioned as transport 1941; renamed U S S WILLIAM P. BIDDLE (APA-8). Laid up in reserve fleet 1946.

309 CITY OF HAVRE
'19, (1931-38) 8,424. Details as (305). Built by Bethlehem Shipbuilding Corp., as VICTORIOUS. Bought by Baltimore Mail Line 1931; renamed CITY OF HAVRE. Transferred to Panama Pacific Line 1938; renamed CITY OF LOS ANGELES. Commissioned as transport 1941; renamed U S S GEORGE F. ELLIOT (AP-13). Sunk by Japanese planes off Guadalcanal, 8 August 1942.

American Scantic Line, New York

310 SCANMAIL
'19, (1932-39) 5,163. 401 x 54. Single screw, turbines, 13 knots. Built by American International Shipbuilding Corp., Hog Island, Pennsylvania, as CHICKASAW for U.S. Shipping Board. Bought by American Scantic Line 1929 and refitted to carry 90 passengers 1932; renamed SCANMAIL. Sold to Lloyd Brasiliero (Brazil) 1940; renamed CAYRU. Torpedoed and sunk off Long Island, 8 March 1942.

311 SCANPENN
'19, (1932-39) 5,163. Details as (310). Built at Hog Island as BIRD CITY. Bought by American Scantic Line 1929. Refitted 1932; renamed SCANPENN. Sold to Lloyd Brasiliero 1940; renamed BUARQUE. Torpedoed and sunk off Cape Hatteras, 15 February 1942.

312 SCANSTATES
'19, (1932-39) 5,163. Details as (310). Built at Hog Island as SAGUACHE. Bought by American Scantic Line 1929. Refitted 1932; renamed SCANSTATES. Sold to Lloyd Brasiliero 1940; renamed CANTUARIA. Withdrawn from service 1958.

313 SCANYORK
'19, (1932-39) 5,163. Details as (310). Built at Hog Island as SCHENECTADY. Bought by American Scantic Line 1929. Refitted 1932; renamed SCANYORK. Sold to Lloyd Brasiliero 1940; renamed MAUA. Constructive total loss 1952.

NETHERLANDS

Holland-America Line

314 MAASDAM (III)
'21, (1934-41) 8,812. 466 x 58. Single screw, turbines, 13 knots. Built by Wilton-Fijenoord, Schiedam. for Cuba-Mexico service. Rebuilt with one funnel and berths reduced to 90, 1934; transferred to North Atlantic service. Torpedoed and sunk in mid-Atlantic, 26 June 1941.

315 EDAM
'21, (1934-54) 8,871. Details as (314). Built by De Schelde Koninklijke Maatschappij, Flushing. Rebuilt 1934; transferred to North Atlantic service. Broken up Hong Kong 1954.

316 LEERDAM
'21, (1934-54) 8,854. Details as (314). Built by Nieuwe Waterweg, Schiedam. Rebuilt 1934; transferred to North Atlantic service. Broken up Japan 1954.

317 SPAARNDAM
'22, (1934-39) 8,857. Details as (314). Built by Nieuwe Waterweg. Laid up Rotterdam 1931-34. Rebuilt 1934; transferred to North Atlantic service. Sunk by magnetic mine in Thames Estuary, 27 November 1939.

Oranje Line

318 PRINS WILLEM VAN ORANJE
'53, (1953-64) 7,328. 462 x 62. Single screw, motorship, 18 knots. Built by Boel's Schweeps-werven, Bolnes. 60 passengers. M.V. Rotterdam-Montreal, 21 September 1953. Sold to V.E.B.

Deutsche Seereederie (East Germany) as training ship 1964; renamed FERDINAND FREILIGRATH.

Trans-Ocean Steamship Co. The Hague

319 ZUIDERKRUIS
'44, (1951-63) 9,376. 455 x 62. Single screw, turbines, 15 knots. Built by Oregon Shipbuilding Corp., Portland as CRANSTON VICTORY. Bought by Dutch Government as emigrant ship 1947 and refitted to carry 900 passengers; renamed ZUIDERKRUIS. F.V. Rotterdam-Quebec, July 1951. Transferred to Trans-Ocean Steamship Co 1960. Sold to Royal Netherlands Navy 1963. Broken up Bilbao 1969.

320 GROOTE BEER
'44, (1952-63) 9,829. Details as (319). Built by Permanente Metals Corp., Richmond, California as COSTA RICA VICTORY. Bought by Dutch Government 1947; renamed GROOTE BEER. F.V. Rotterdam-Quebec, July 1952. Transferred to Trans-Ocean Steamship Co 1960. Sold to John S. Latsis (Greece) 1963. Renamed MARIANNA IV 1964; renamed GROOTE BEER 1965; renamed MARIANNA IV 1968. Laid up Piraeus November 1968; broken up Eleusis, Greece 1970.

321 WATERMAN (I)
'45, (1952-63) 9,900. Details as (319). Built by Oregon Shipbuilding Corp. as LA GRANDE VICTORY. Bought by Dutch Government 1947; renamed WATERMAN. F.V. Rotterdam-Quebec, July 1952. Transferred to Trans-Ocean Steamship Co 1960. Sold to John S. Latsis 1963; renamed MARGARITA. Laid up at Shimotsu, Japan, February 1969; broken up Hiroshima 1970.

DENMARK

East Asiatic Company, Copenhagen

322 JUTLANDIA
'34, (1946-50) 8,457. 460 x 61. Twin screw, motorship, 15 knots. Built by Nakskov Skibsvaerft Nakskov. 69 passengers. Operated in Far East service. Transferred to Copenhagen-New York service 1946. Converted to hospital ship for service in Korea 1950. Broken up Bilbao 1965.

323 ERRIA
'32, (1949-51) 7,670. 463 x 62. Twin screw, motorship, 16 knots. Built by Nakskov Skibsvaerft 74 passengers. Transferred to Copenhagen-New York service 1949; returned to Far East service two years later. Broken up Osaka 1962.

324 FALSTRIA
'45, (1951-53) 8,482. 453 x 63. Single screw, motorship, 16 knots. Built by Nakskov Skibsvaerft 64 passengers. Transferred to Copenhagen-New York service 1951; returned to Far East service 1953. Sold to Empajada Cia. Navegacion (Greece) 1964; renamed VERYR, Broken up Onimichi, Japan 1964.

YUGOSLAVIA

Jugolinija, Rijeka

325 HRVATSKA
'45, (1949-66) 7,909. 455 x 62. Single screw, turbines, 17 knots. Built by Permanente Metals Corp.,

Richmond, California, as ST LAWRENCE VICTORY. Bought by Jugolinija and refitted to carry 60 passengers 1948; renamed ZAGREB. Renamed HRVATSKA 1949. F.V. Rijeka-New York, 20 September 1949. Sold to Cia. Nav. Adriatica S.A. (Burundi) 1966.

326 SRBIJA
'49, (1949-66) 6,634. 475 x 60. Single screw, motorship, 15 knots. Launched by Rotterdamsche Droogdok Maatschappij, Rotterdam, as CROSTAFELS; completed to modified design as DRVAR by A. Vuyk & Zonen, Yssel, 1949. 44 passengers. Renamed SRBIJA 1949. F.V. Rijeka-New York, 12 October 1949. Passenger berths reduced to twelve 1966. Sold to Soc. d' Avances Commerciales S.A. (Somali Republic) 1968; renamed ARMELLE.

327 VISEVECA ●
'64, (1964-   ) 7,759. 489 x 67. Single screw, motorship, 18 knots. Built by Brodogradiliste 3 Maj, Rijeka. 50 passengers. M.V. Rijeka-New York 1964.

328 TUHOBIC ●
'65, (1965-   ) 7,759. Details as (327). Built by Brodogradiliste 3 Maj. M.V. Rijeka-New York 1965.

329 KLEK ●
'65, (1965-   ) 7,759. Details as (327). Built by Brodogradiliste 3 Maj . M.V. Rijeka-New York 1965.

330 ZVIR ●
'65, (1965-   ) 7,760. Details as (327). Built by Brodogradiliste 3 Maj. M.V. Rijeka-New York 1965.

Splosna Plovba, Piran

331 BLED
'45, (1959-62) 7,714. 448 x 57. Single screw, motorship, 14 knots. Laid down 1940 by J. Cockerill S.A. Hoboken, as ALEX VAN OPSTAL for Cie. Maritime Belge (Belgium). Construction halted by war. Seized by Germans upon completion 1945; renamed KANONIER. Recovered in Baltic after war and renamed ALEX VAN OPSTAL. Bought by Splosna Plovba and refitted to carry 60 passengers 1959; renamed BLED. Transferred to West Africa service 1962. Passenger berths reduced to twelve 1968. Broken up La Spezia 1970.

332 BOVEC
'45, (1959-62) 7,724. Details as (331). Laid down 1940 by J. Cockerill as ARMAND GRISAR for Cie. Maritime Belge. Scuttled by retreating Germans 1944; raised and completed 1945. Bought by Splosna Plovba 1959; renamed BOVEC. Transferred to West Africa service 1962. Passenger berths reduced to twelve 1968. Broken up Whampoa, China 1970.

333 BOHINJ
'46, (1959-62) 7,724. Details as (331). Laid down 1940 by J. Cockerill as GOUVERNEUR GALOPIN for Cie. Maritime Belge. Scuttled 1944; raised and completed 1946. Bought by Splosna Plovba 1959; renamed BOHINJ. Transferred to West Africa service 1962. Passenger berths reduced to twelve 1968.

UNITED ARAB REPUBLIC

United Arab Maritime Co, Alexandria

334 CLEOPATRA ●
'44, (1948-) 8,193. 455 x 62. Single screw, turbines, 14 knots. Built by Oregon Shipbuilding
Corp., Portland, Oregon, as UNITED VICTORY. Bought by Khedivial Mail Line (Egypt) and
refitted to carry 78 passengers 1947; renamed KHEDIVE ISMAIL. F.V. Alexandria-New York,
15 March 1948. Renamed CLEOPATRA 1956. Transferred to United Arab Maritime Co 1962.

335 SALAH EL DIN
'44, (1948-63) 8,199. Details as (334). Built by Californian Shipbuilding Corp., Los Angeles, as
ATCHISON VICTORY. Bought by Khedivial Mail Line and refitted 1947; renamed MOHAMED
ALI EL KEBIR. F.V. Alexandria-New York, 1948. Renamed SALAH EL DIN 1960. Transferred
to United Arab Maritime Co 1962. Sold to Salvador Investment Co. (Liberia) 1963; renamed
MERCANTILE VICTORY. Broken up Castellon, Spain, 1965.

336 STAR OF SUEZ ●
'48, (1964-) 6,240. 408 x 57. Single screw, motorship, 14 knots. Built by Cantieri Riuniti dell'
Adriatico, Trieste, for Alexandria Navigation Co (Egypt). 40 passengers. Transferred to United
Arab Maritime Co 1962. F.V. Alexandria-Montreal, 1964.

APPENDIX 1

THE TWENTY FIVE LARGEST SHIPS IN ORDER OF OVERALL LENGTH

		NAME	YEAR	LINE	O.L.	G.R.T.
*	1	FRANCE	1962	French Line	1035	66,348
	2	QUEEN ELIZABETH	1940	Cunard Line	1031	83,673
	3	NORMANDIE	1935	French Line	1027	82,799
	4	QUEEN MARY	1936	Cunard Line	1020	81,237
	5	UNITED STATES	1952	United States Lines	990	53,329
*	6	QUEEN ELIZABETH 2	1969	Cunard Line	963	65,863
	7	MAJESTIC	1922	White Star Line	956	56,551
	8	LEVIATHAN	1914	United States Lines	950	54,282
	9	LIBERTE	1930	French Line	938	51,839
	10	BREMEN	1929	Norddeutscher Lloyd	938	51,656
	11	BERENGARIA	1913	Cunard Line	919	52,002
*	12	RAFFAELLO	1965	Italian Line	905	45,933
*	13	MICHELANGELO	1965	Italian Line	905	45,911
	14	AQUITANIA	1914	Cunard Line	902	45,647
	15	OLYMPIC	1911	White Star Line	883	46,439
	16	TITANIC	1912	White Star Line	882	46,329
	17	REX	1932	Italian Line	879	51,062
	18	CONTE DI SAVOIA	1932	Italian Line	814	48,502
	19	ILE DE FRANCE	1927	French Line	792	44,356
	20	MAURETANIA (I)	1907	Cunard Line	790	31,938
	21	LUSITANIA	1907	Cunard Line	790	31,550
*	22	OCEANIC	1965	Home Lines	782	39,241
	23	HOMERIC	1922	White Star Line	774	34,351
	24	MAURETANIA (II)	1939	Cunard Line	771	35,738
	25	PARIS	1921	French Line	765	34,569

SHIPS BUILT UNDER ANOTHER NAME

MAJESTIC	ex	BISMARCK	Hamburg American Line
LEVIATHAN		VATERLAND	Hamburg American Line
LIBERTE		EUROPA	Norddeutscher Lloyd
BERENGARIA		IMPERATOR	Hamburg American Line

* SHIPS IN SERVICE 1971

APPENDIX 2

RECORD PASSAGES: VESSELS IN SERVICE AFTER 1925

WESTBOUND

YEAR	SHIP	LINE	DAY-HR-MIN	MILES	KNOTS
1909	MAURETANIA	Cunard Line	4 . 10 . 51	2,784	26.06 (1)
1929	BREMEN	Nord. Lloyd	4 . 17 . 42	3,164	27.83 (2)
1930	EUROPA	Nord. Lloyd	4 . 17 . 6	3,157	27.91 (2)
1933	BREMEN	Nord. Lloyd	4 . 16 . 15	3,199	28.51 (2)
1933	REX	Italian Line	4 . 13 . 58	3,181	29.92 (3)
1935	NORMANDIE	French Line	4 . 3 . 2	2,971	29.98 (4)
1936	QUEEN MARY	Cunard Line	4 . 0 . 27	2,907	30.14 (4)
1937	NORMANDIE	French Line	3 . 23 . 2	2,906	30.58 (4)
1938	QUEEN MARY	Cunard Line	3 . 21 . 48	2,907	30.99 (4)
1952	UNITED STATES	United States Lines	3 . 12 . 12	2,906	34.51 (4)

(1)   DAUNT'S ROCK - SANDY HOOK
(2)   CHERBOURG - AMBROSE LIGHT
(3)   GIBRALTAR - AMBROSE LIGHT
(4)   BISHOP ROCK - AMBROSE LIGHT

EASTBOUND

YEAR	SHIP	LINE	DAY-HR-MIN	MILES	KNOTS
1924	MAURETANIA	Cunard Line	4 . 19 . 0	3,008	26.16 (1)
1929	BREMEN	Nord. Lloyd	4 . 14 . 30	3,084	27.92 (2)
1935	NORMANDIE	French Line	4 . 3 . 28	3,015	30.31 (3)
1936	QUEEN MARY	Cunard Line	3 . 23 . 57	2,939	30.63 (3)
1937	NORMANDIE	French Line	4 . 0 . 6	2,978	30.99 (3)
1937	NORMANDIE	French Line	3 . 22 . 7	2,936	31.30 (3)
1938	QUEEN MARY	Cunard Line	3 . 20 . 42	2,938	31.69 (3)
1952	UNITED STATES	United States Lines	3 . 10 . 40	2,942	35.59 (3)

(1)   AMBROSE LIGHT - CHERBOURG
(2)   AMBROSE LIGHT - EDDYSTONE LIGHT
(3)   AMBROSE LIGHT - BISHOP ROCK

APPENDIX 3

ATLANTIC LINERS IN SERVICE BEFORE 1925; LISTED IN INDEX UNDER LATER NAMES

NAME AND *LISTED NAME*	LINE	NO.
ALSATIAN '14 *EMPRESS OF FRANCE (I)*	Allan	70
AMERIKA '05 *AMERICA*	Hamburg American	102
BERLIN (I) '08 *ARABIC (III)*	Norddeutscher Lloyd	44
BLUCHER '02 *SUFFREN*	Hamburg American	189
COMMONWEALTH '00 *CANOPIC*	Dominion	39
CRETIC '03 *DEVONIAN (II)*	White Star	65
CZAR '12 *ESTONIA*	Russian American	255
CZARITZA '12 *LITUANIA*	Russian American	256
EMPRESS OF BRITAIN (I) '06 *MONTROYAL*	Canadian Pacific	66
EMPRESS OF INDIA '21 *MONTNAIRN*	Canadian Pacific	74
HANOVERIAN '02 *DEVONIAN (II)*	Leyland	65
IMPERATOR '13 *BERENGARIA*	Hamburg American	5
KAISER FRANZ JOSEF I '12 *PRESIDENTE WILSON*	Unione Austriaca	130
KAISERIN AUGUSTE VICTORIA '06 *EMPRESS OF SCOTLAND (I)*	Hamburg American	75
KONIG FRIEDRICH AUGUST '06 *MONTREAL (II)*	Hamburg American	73
KONIGIN LUISE '96 *EDISON*	Norddeutscher Lloyd	225
KURSK '10 *POLONIA*	Russian American	264
MAYFLOWER '03 *DEVONIAN (II)*	Dominion	65
MEGALI HELLAS '20 *BYRON*	National Steam Nav.	224

MONTLAURIER '22 *MONTNAIRN*	Canadian Pacific	74
PITTSBURGH '22 *PENNLAND*	White Star	58
POTSDAM '00 *STOCKHOLM (1)*	Holland-America	237
PRESIDENT GRANT '07 *REPUBLIC*	Hamburg American	107
PRESIDENT PIERCE '22 *PRESIDENT ROOSEVELT*	United States	104
PRESIDENT TAFT '22 *PRESIDENT HARDING*	United States	104
PRINZ FRIEDRICH WILHELM '08 *MONTNAIRN*	Norddeutscher Lloyd	74
TUNISIAN '00 *MARBURN*	Allan	68
TYRRHENIAN '22 *LANCASTRIA*	Cunard	12
VATERLAND '14 *LEVIATHAN*	Hamburg American	106
VICTORIAN '05 *MARLOCH*	Allan	69
VIRGINIAN '05 *DROTTNINGHOLM*	Allan	238

LIST OF SOURCES

Baker, W.A. and Tre Tryckare   The Engine Powered Vessel
Bonsor, N.R.P.   North Atlantic Seaway
Dunn, Laurence   Passenger Liners 1961, 1965
North Atlantic Liners
Ship Recognition, Liners
Famous Liners of the Past, Belfast Built
Gibbs, C.R. Vernon   Passenger Liners of the Western Ocean
British Passenger Liners of the Five Oceans
Isherwood, J.H.   Steamers of the Past
Sea Breezes Famous Ships
Le Fleming, H.M.   Ships of the Holland-America Line
Musk, George   Canadian Pacific 1891-1961
Newell, Gordon   Ocean Liners of the Twentieth Century
Schwadtke, J.-H   Deutschlands Handelsflotte 1964, 1968
Smith, Eugene W.   Passenger Ships of the World, Past and Present
Talbot-Booth, E.C.   Merchant Ships 1942, 1949-50, 1959, 1963

Periodicals

Fairplay International Shipping Journal
Marine News
Merchant Ships, World Built
The Motor Ship
Sea Breezes
Ships Illustrated

INDEX OF SHIPS

SHIPS LISTED IN INDEX UNDER TWO OR MORE NAMES